THE UNIVERSITY OF MICHIGAN
CENTER FOR JAPANESE STUDIES

MICHIGAN PAPERS IN JAPANESE STUDIES
NO. 7

INDUSTRY AT THE CROSSROADS

edited by

Robert E. Cole

Ann Arbor

Center for Japanese Studies
The University of Michigan

1982

*Open access edition funded by the National Endowment for the Humanities/
Andrew W. Mellon Foundation Humanities Open Book Program.*

ISBN 0-939512-12-2

Printed and bound by CPI Group (UK) Ltd, Croydon, CR0 4YY

ISBN 978-0-939512-12-6 (paper)
ISBN 978-0-472-88013-3 (ebook)
ISBN 978-0-472-90204-0 (open access)

TABLE OF CONTENTS

Preface

The "mood" of a conference can tell us a great deal about the state of mind pervading an industry. The mood of our first U. S.-Japan Auto Conference in January 1981 could only be described as electric. People wanted to know what our problems were and how we could begin to solve them. Inherent in the latter issue was the question, what could we learn from the Japanese? One left the conference with a sense that there was a call for action, a mandate to address the problems facing the industry.

The mood, about a year later, at our March 1982 U. S.-Japan Auto Conference was far more subdued. While undoubtedly this reflected the stream of statistics confirming the continually depressed state of the industry, we would like to think that another dynamic was operating as well. Whereas the 1981 conference was "electric," a state of mind which flowed from a certain frustration at seemingly overwhelming difficulties and often vague expectations of what we might learn from the Japanese, the 1982 conference was more "workmanlike" in the sense that speakers discussed specifically what progress was being made in addressing problems. This more subdued, pragmatic approach continued throughout and was reinforced by the workshops held the day after the main conference.

Instead of discussing the virtues of the Just-in-Time system in Japan, we addressed the practical problems of introducing such a system in U. S. firms. Instead of railing about the benefits or failings of regulation of the industry, we discussed what we could reasonably expect from regulation. Instead of exhorting the industry to adopt Japanese practices willy-nilly, we focused on some of the limitations of the Japanese model in a range of different areas. Instead of trying to identify some magic key to Japanese success in the automotive industry, we discussed the interrelationships among various factors. At the same time, we continued to explore the basic issues transforming the auto industry worldwide. In this connection, we sought to unravel some of the complexities associated with the internationalization of the auto industry and trade obligations under the GATT.

vii

To be sure, the second conference may not have provided the same excitement as the first one. Yet we believe that more was accomplished in terms of our educational mission.

I would like once again to thank Harold Shapiro, President of the University, for his strong support for our efforts. The Planning Committee was composed of: David E. Cole, Director of the Office for the Study of Automotive Transportation; Susan Lipschutz, Assistant to the President of the University; Donald N. Smith, Director of the Industrial Development Division of the Institute of Science and Technology; Alfred S. Sussman, Dean of the Horace H. Rackham School of Graduate Studies; and myself. We also benefited greatly from the advice of our Advisory Board, composed of: Donald F. Ephlin, Vice President and Director of the National Ford Department, United Auto Workers; David S. Potter, Vice President and Group Executive of Public Affairs Group, General Motors Corporation; Fred G. Secrest, Consultant and former Executive Vice President, Ford Motor Company; and Leonard Woodcock, Adjunct Professor of Political Science, the University of Michigan.

Downs Herold provided invaluable professional guidance in organizing the conference, and Donna Welton, the Conference Coordinator, performed admirably.

Robert E. Cole
Professor of Sociology
Project Director, Joint U. S.-Japan Automotive Study
University of Michigan

INTRODUCTION

Harold T. Shapiro

On behalf of the Regents, the Executive Officers, and the faculty of the University, it is my great pleasure to welcome you to today's conference. I want to extend a special welcome to the speakers and discussion leaders who will play such a critical role in the conference. The University of Michigan is proud to have started what is now a series of conferences on an important and timely subject. We are proud to have served, at least in part, as a catalyst for focusing discussion on a very important problem, the automotive industry in the United States and Japan.

I am particularly attracted by the nature of the title for this conference, "Industry at the Crossroads." An industrial economy, such as we have had since World War II, is always at the crossroads. One of the characteristics of a market economy is that there are constant tensions. These tensions are not necessarily symptoms of a disease; these tensions are, more often than not, symptoms of the market's discipline as it tries to allocate production to the most efficient producers. So, in the rapidly changing world in which we now find ourselves, industry, and especially modern industry, is always at a crossroads.

In this latter respect industry is analogous to quality higher education. In my Inaugural Address in 1980 I said that, for a very similar reason, quality education is always at a crossroads. The world around us is a dynamic one and if we do not change with it we will be left behind. There is an anecdote which is told about a football coach, Woody Hayes at Ohio State University. They claim that once, when he was a bit aggravated, he told one of the players, "Look, you're either getting better or you're getting worse." And while I would not like to be a football player playing under that exhortation, there is something to it both in the worlds of higher education and of industry. You are either getting better or you are getting worse; you are either leading the pack or falling back. In a dynamic economy, such as we have today, comparative advantage is always changing. There is, and

Harold T. Shapiro is Professor of Economics and Public Policy and President of The University of Michigan.

1

should be, therefore, a continuous shifting in the international distribution of production in manufacturing and in other areas.

Why is it appropriate that this issue of the shifting international distribution of production, the changing configuration of industry in various parts of the world, be discussed at a university? It is appropriate for a number of reasons, but I will mention only one. The university, as I see it, has a dual role in society. First of all, it is society's servant. We have to train people in the skills society wants: doctors, lawyers, engineers, accountants, and many others. We perform the function of passing on the accumulated knowledge of our civilization and, in that sense, we also serve as a servant of society. However, there is another important role of the university which places it in a very sensitive relationship to society. It is also our responsibility to serve as society's critic. What does that mean in the context of this conference? It is a university's responsibility to think of alternative visions of the world, and to remind us that the world as we find it today is just one possible case. If we are going to grow, in the broadest sense of that word—not simply economic growth but growth as a civilization—we must consider alternative ways of doing things. Others usually face those alternative visions only in a time of crisis or semicrisis. A university must do this constantly if it is to meet its full responsibilities to society. That is why I am glad that the University of Michigan is serving as host to these conferences and why I thank my colleagues who have put this conference together.

In the industry that will be the focal point of much of your attention, there have been dramatic changes, and it is obviously time for the consideration of alternative visions. It is also time to try to fit whatever solutions we think are appropriate into the broad scope of the world economy. If the world economy is going to be productive and enable mankind as a whole to fulfill its social agenda, we cannot be parochial in our solutions to these problems. If there are important changes and difficult transitions to be made, we must face up to them and deal with them as best we can. It is a challenging time for the automotive industry in the United States and, in particular, for the state of Michigan. Even for the country as a whole, there is much at stake. Nonetheless, I hope that your discussions will be characterized by a sense of participation, not simply in what is going on here in Michigan, not simply in what is going on in the United States, but in what is going on in the world economy. The solutions you derive for these problems will have to take into account your responsibilities to this state and nation and also to a much wider set of humanity. I wish you all the best of luck, and I hope we will see you back at the University of Michigan often.

OPENING STATEMENT

Paul W. McCracken

That it is appropriate and urgent for a conference on this subject to be taking place in Michigan would seem to be obvious enough. This state and the automotive and associated industries now have the dubious distinction of leading the nation in one economic yardstick—namely, the unemployment rate. And the questions confronting these companies are awesome in their uncertainty and magnitude.

This industry has always been hyper-responsive to cyclical swings in the economy at large, as is clearly indicated by data in Table 1. From the third quarter of 1974 to the first quarter of 1975, for example, output for the economy as a whole (in real terms) declined 3.4 percent, but the auto component of real GNP dropped 28.3 percent. During the first year of the expansion, however, incomes and output nationally (again in real terms) rose 6.7 percent, historically about an average recovery, but the auto component of real GNP rose 55 percent. During the first year of recovery after the 1957-58 recession real GNP rose 8.4 percent and the auto component rose 44.4 percent.

This historical record does carry with it a message of hope. The economy is again today in a recession (an announcement which I make since many of you here today may not be aware of these things). If we are close to another upturn for the economy generally, which would be in line with our historical experience, and if the auto industry's response to improving business conditions were in line with our cyclical history, this industry could then anticipate a sharp improvement in the year or so ahead.

While for this industry the difference between a rising economy generally and a declining one continues to be important, and that in itself should be the harbinger of better things down the road, it also seems clear that the industry is

Paul W. McCracken is Edmund Ezra Day Distinguished University Professor of Business Administration, The University of Michigan, and Chairman, Council of Academic Advisers, American Enterprise Institute for Public Policy Research.

confronting adjustments and uncertainties far more fundamental than simply being on the end of the usual cyclical whipcracker. Our problems did not begin in July 1981 when business activity generally turned downward. The fork in the road which this industry has reached is far more basic than surviving yet another recession.

Table 1

CHANGE IN REAL GNP
AND IN THE AUTO INDUSTRY COMPONENT OF REAL GNP
DURING RECESSIONS AND RECOVERIES

Recession	During Decline		First Year of Recovery	
	GNP	Auto	GNP	Auto
1957-58	-3.3%	-26.4%	+6.9%	+24.7%
1960-61	-1.2	-16.0	+6.4	+5.6
1969-70	-1.0	-21.4	+2.8	+32.7
1974-75	-3.4	-28.3	+6.7	+55.0

Source: Basic data from the U. S. Department of Commerce. All percentage figures are computed from data in 1972 prices.

The decade of the 1970s concluded with one of those discontinuites that are rare in economic history—a sudden internationalization of the auto market. With the collapse of Iran an important component of the world's oil supply was interrupted. Our government, through its control of prices that largely denied us access to world supplies in the spot market, concentrated a disproportionate share of the world shortage on the United States—the usual tendency to shoot ourselves in the foot with government management of markets.

The American auto market, which for years had been moving back toward the larger cars in which our industry had specialized, ran to the small-car side of the deck. Our market was no longer a "privileged sanctuary" created by the preference of most (though not all) Americans for cars of a size made largely in the United States. What the American market then seemed to want were cars with which companies outside this country had more experience and immediate capacity than ours here at home.

The magnitude of questions and problems posed for our industry by this sudden, almost discontinuous, internationalization was awesome. Enormous capital outlays were required during a period of hemorrhaging losses. Costs were found to be higher here by a larger margin than could be explained by, for example, the rapidly narrowing differential between per capita incomes generally in Japan and the United States. Precisely the developments forcing companies to factor internationalization into their thinking—about markets, production, and suppliers—were also producing massive strains and imbalances courting the growing risk of heading the trading world in a protectionist direction (a direction which, once set, is not easily reversed). After deploying capital and management energy on the basis of an international strategy, will companies find themselves impeded by growing trade barriers? With scarce capital resources heavily committed to down-sized cars (forced partly by our mishandling the last oil shortage, and partly by legislative mandate), are buyers, in effect, now going to say: "We've changed our minds and after all prefer larger cars"?

Clearly the industry is at crossroads where managements must make decisions that bet the net worth of their companies on the direction to be taken. By the close of this conference we shall not confidently have answered all the questions, but the questions we are addressing are not trivial.

NEW DIRECTIONS IN
AUTO TRANSPORTATION POLICY

Mark G. Aron

You may wonder why it's appropriate for a railroad lawyer to be talking about Japan and autos. As my biography indicates, however, I spent almost nine years at the Department of Transportation in Washington. Although I did not work for the National Highway Traffic Safety Administration (NHTSA) directly, I was involved with many particular NHTSA activities and with transportation regulation in general. I should indicate before proceeding further that what follow are my personal observations.

Hopefully my distance from the NHTSA process gives me some objectivity, if it is possible to be objective about NHTSA. Today I'd like to discuss the NHTSA experience, especially the safety rules, because it is both important in itself and a case study of how the regulatory process works and perhaps how it doesn't work. My objective is to convince you to approach NHTSA and the regulatory process with less emotionalism and less of a partisan spirit. Because of an emotional overreaction, the present process has been radically politicized, and this direction will cause us all future difficulties.

In looking at almost any regulatory process, there seems to be a lot of myth and legend, and NHTSA is no exception. The NHTSA legend goes something like this.

In the 1960s, Congress, in its great wisdom and after long and arduous review, enacted a statute with a clear and unambiguous mandate for regulation of motor vehicle safety. When that statute was passed, everyone anticipated what regulations would be issued, but Congress thought certain details had to be worked out by the technocrats.

The technocrats . . . or bureaucrats as they would later be called . . . slowly at first, but later with increasing abandon, issued more and more regulations, with

Mark G. Aron is Assistant General Counsel, CSX Corporation.

total disregard for the congressional direction. A classic case of a bureaucracy thwarting the will of Congress. During Republican administrations and during a few sessions of Congress, attempts were made to chastise the bureaucracy and to slow this process, but under the most recent Democratic administration, all attempts at regulatory restraint were abandoned. And to make matters worse . . . and since this is myth . . . a wicked witch from the East, Joan by name, whipped the little munchkins into an utter frenzy of rulemaking.

Ah, but help was on the way, because out of the West came a shining white knight (and I decided to use that term even before I read Senator Packwood's recent remarks) who slew the wicked witch and riffed the munchkins. And we all lived happily ever after or something like that.

As in all myths, there are elements of truth, but there are also very significant departures from the truth.

During the 1960s, there was a tremendous outpouring of public sentiment for some action in the auto safety area. Many states acted on their own to enact very tough anti-drunk-driving and speed laws. I grew up in Connecticut and then-Governor Abraham Ribicoff made his early political reputation by instituting a very rigorous anti-speed and drunk-driving campaign. Other states followed.

But there was a call for action on the federal level. Let me quote from one early report to give you a feeling for the tenor of the times:

> Death on the nation's highways hit an all-time high (last year) when an estimated 55,500 people died in motor vehicle crashes. . . . If unchecked, motor vehicle crashes will produce at least a quarter million fatalities on our highways in the next four years. . . .
> The grim statistics unmistakenly highlight that in motor vehicle deaths, the nation faces a destructive problem equal in size and complexity to other social ills such as crime, disease and poverty. . . . Highway injuries exceeded by ten times violent criminal acts combined. . . . Motor vehicle crashes rob society of nearly as many productive working years as heart disease and of more than are lost to cancer and strokes.

Some might anticipate this quotation emanated from Ralph Nader. Actually, it comes from the second annual highway safety report which was submitted by President Richard Nixon. It gives some idea of the impetus for the regulation. These regulations didn't spring without reason from the brain of a mindless clerk in Washington. The public definitely perceived a need. And it is important to understand that support *for* regulation (and in fact support for later regulatory reform) was bipartisan in nature. If the regulations were excessive, they were more related to the times than to the party.

Congress reacted to this pressure by enacting the National Traffic and Motor Vehicle Safety Act of 1966. Far from giving specific directions to what was to become NHTSA, this act simply stated that the Department of Transportation (DOT) was to establish *"appropriate* Federal motor vehicle safety standards." They were to be "practicable . . . meet the needs for motor vehicle safety . . . and be stated in objective terms." "Motor vehicle safety" was defined in terms of "unreasonable risk." Except for a few admonitions to "consider" relevant safety data, the act provided little guidance. It did not mention cost-benefit analysis in the text, and it did not pinpoint specific areas for regulation. In fact, although it is a somewhat controversial issue, there were references in the statutory history that indicated that DOT was not to make use of cost-benefit analysis as the sole regulatory determinant. A cost-benefit requirement was considered but then not adopted in the original debate. Many of the earlier administrators at NHTSA and some members of Congress read the statute as requiring NHTSA to issue any regulation that was technologically feasible and advanced safety.

Actually, the NHTSA statute was not that different from other transportation safety statutes. If one compares the Federal Aviation Act, the Hazardous Materials Transportation Act, the various pipeline safety acts, or the Federal Rail Safety Act, one will find, to a fairly similar degree, requirements to issue appropriate or reasonable safety regulations with little or no further guidance.

If one is looking for villains in this process (if there are any villains), one has to be tempted to place at least some of the blame for any excessive regulation on the Congress. It was the Congress which started this process. Later when public opinion shifted, as in the interlock situation, the Congress would rise in righteous indignation and claim the agency had violated Congress's express intentions. But this would be a false claim since rarely did the Congress give any real guidance to the agency except "to do good."

Once the statute was passed, the regulatory process moved with amazing speed and, at least in this initial period, with little controversy. The great bulk of NHTSA safety regulation occurred in the very early days of the program. Again, let us realize that we are talking of rule making during the first few years of the Nixon administration. One of the first moves of that administration was to increase the status of the agency dealing with motor vehicle safety and to make it an agency. Quoting from the Third Annual Report, this elevation in the status of NHTSA was needed "to accelerate highway safety progress and emphasize the national importance of the problem."

As accomplishments, that report listed the issuance of twenty-nine motor vehicle safety standards and the proposal of an additional ninety-five standards. It also bragged that the first fines were levied at vehicle manufacturers for not complying with vehicle safety standards. The goal of this program was "to make breakthroughs in vehicle crash protection and control of abnormal driving behavior."

It is true that many of these regulations were based upon existing GSA standards and existing technology, but one should still not undervalue the immensity of this early program. Reading through the list of regulations and proposals gives some idea as to its breadth: one regulation for transmissions; six regulations dealing with windshields; one for mirrors; seven regulations for brakes; five regulations for tires; two for bumpers; individual regulations for steering, seat belts, exterior protrusions, door latches, fuel tanks, radiator caps, jacks, and odometers. Many of these areas would become controversial. On June 26, 1969, DOT issued an Advanced Notice of Proposed Rulemaking for "an inflatable passive restraint system" to be required on new cars in 1972. The next few years would in fact see the first automatic passive restraint system requirements, an interlock requirement, the truck braking rule (121), early bumper standards, and the first tire-grading system—a heavy rate of activity and all prior to 1976.

Many have seen the period after 1976 as a time when regulation reached a frenzy; but in many respects, except for fuel economy, which was a new mandated activity thrust upon NHTSA, the non-safety bumper rules, and the reinstatement of the passive restraint requirement, little new regulation was instituted. There were some new rules, but many of them were marginal in importance. Several proposals were made just before the close of the Carter administration, but they were more gestures of contempt than serious proposals. In many respects, NHTSA had fulfilled the great bulk of its mission. Some would point to the increase in enforcement after 1976, and depending upon how you analyze it, there was an increase after 1976. But in many respects, the activity of post-1976 was not much greater than the surge of activity in the early 1970s after the initial regulations were issued.

Using the figures from the 1978 Annual Report, in 1970, defect notifications involved less than one million vehicles. In 1971, notifications were directed toward nine million vehicles; and although the pace falls off for 1972 and 1973, between seven and eight million vehicles were recalled. Then the pace further decreases to between two-three million vehicles and rises again to eight-ten million vehicles in 1977 and 1978, figures not that dissimilar from the early 1970s.

I suppose we could discuss the passive restraint issue for the better part of this morning. I don't pretend to be an expert, although as a consumer I did support it. Although the level of real safety regulatory activity did not increase significantly after 1976, there was a decided increase in the level of regulatory rhetoric. It was clear that there existed in the minds of certain of the senior people of NHTSA a "devil type" theory. In other words, the industry was totally unreasonable and worse—it was immoral and evil.

It is one thing to be considered wrong or even unreasonable. It is quite another to be called immoral. Once you say this, you cut off any reasonable discussion and guarantee that the process has to be conducted in the most adversarial fashion.

In the particular case of NHTSA, the industry reacted with its own vehemence and emotion. In the end, NHTSA was totally incapable of rationally reviewing compromise solutions, such as the Coleman contract, which, although flawed in the sense that it had several escape hatches, might have provided the basis for reform. And the industry itself was unable to react rationally. It continued to promote cars with excessive motor power, and the industry in the late 1970s was still denying the legitimacy of the early NHTSA regulation even though it had been accepted by the public. The outside consumer groups and the well-paid attorneys of Connecticut Avenue who represented the industry also did not find it in their respective interests to inject reason into the process. Who is to blame for this situation is unclear. What it does prove is that irrationality begets irrationality. But one should not make the mistake of judging NHTSA solely in light of this period of excessive rhetoric. NHTSA accomplished a great deal, and the great bulk of its regulation was accepted as sensible and needed. Those in the auto industry who would judge NHTSA harshly should be wary lest a similar standard is used to judge the industry itself. NHTSA had its 121 and the industry had its Edsel.

Let me now talk a moment about reform, both past and future. Contrary to some claims, regulatory reform at NHTSA and in general has a long bipartisan foundation. DOT was always in the forefront of regulatory reform. The Ford administration submitted legislation regarding the economic regulation of airlines, railroads, and motor carriers. Interestingly enough, the auto industry and the unions for the most part took either a neutral or negative position with respect to this legislation.

It could be argued that reform of economic regulation was not related to safety and environmental reform, but, at least with the aid of hindsight, to any reasonable observer it had to be clear that reform in the economic area had to spill over to the safety area. In fact, during the Ford period, there was considerable internal reform of safety regulation at DOT. Secretary Coleman early had a policy to review major regulation at a secretarial level. You will remember that it was Secretary Coleman himself who reviewed the passive restraint issue. NHTSA itself adopted a revised procedure to review its own regulation.

Both the economic and safety reforms were continued after 1976. President Carter passed regulatory-reform proposals in the air, rail, and motor areas. Secretary Adams first had a departmental policy and then a more formalized departmental order calling for review of internal legislation. These became some of the basic foundations for the Carter programs that were applied government-wide. And with respect to the auto industry itself, there was a specific study of auto regulations that culminated in Secretary Goldschmidt's auto report, which among other items recommended a "slowing of regulation."

Much of this effort was redone and recast in its own terms by the Reagan administration. In many respects, what we have ended up with, however, is not a rationalization or reform of the regulatory process but a politicization of regulations and what might be called an "impoundment" of the various safety statutes. You will remember that several years ago the Executive branch, without attempting to go to Congress to change the laws, refused to spend money Congress had directed to be spent—in other words, the Executive impounded the money. I fear this is what has occurred with the most recent regulatory changes. Without seeking a basic statutory change, the Executive has, for the most part, ceased engaging in new regulatory activity. The process is a problem, but the end result is just as troublesome.

Let me stress, however, just as reform had a bipartisan history, impoundment also has a bipartisan foundation. The Carter program had many of the same elements as the Reagan procedures. It is just not clear, however, whether the Carter administration intended to go so far with its activities.

We have come to this stage because of the product of two trends: excessive reliance on cost-benefit analysis and an excessive centralization of the regulatory process. These are two main points of the Reagan regulatory program. Cost-benefit analysis is a valuable tool. No one denies that there are scarce resources in our society or that we have to weigh the benefits and cost of particular proposals. The problem is to what degree we rely upon cost-benefit analysis as a determinant of regulatory policy. If we say that to issue any regulation one must prove, with a significant degree of exactness, that the benefits of a regulation exceed the costs—and we set up as judge an administration that is philosophically opposed to regulation (and that is the case we have today)—we won't have much regulation. Benefits are difficult to quantify. How much is a human life worth? How much is a child's life worth? How accurate is our data base in terms of less philosophical items? How many crashes occur between 2.5 mph and 5.0 mph? Costs are dependent in large part on market responses. How many consumers will buy air bags? How aggressively will car companies market safety? If you require that a benefit be proven beyond a shadow of a doubt and in light of all this uncertainty, the regulation must fail the test. Reasonable men can disagree. But that does not mean that the rule is unreasonable. Many times cost-benefit analysis serves as a rationalization for an already agreed-upon result. In a nice touch of irony, in the most recent procedures involving passive restraints, it was the proponents of the passive restraints that argued for a cost-benefit analysis and the industry who argued that other factors should be weighed.

Can seventy-five GS-14s in the Office of Management and Budget (OMB) run the federal government's regulatory program? Under current procedures, the great bulk of government regulation must pass OMB approval. If one makes the passageway narrow enough, very few will be able to move through it. In this case, we don't have a doorway—we have the proverbial eye of the needle. With such limited staff, the responses are predictable. The easiest answer for an over-worked OMB reviewer is to simply pile the regulations up on his or her desk and give no answer or to deny approval to all regulations. This happened initially. The next response is to deny an arbitrary percentage of regulations, say 10 percent. This was also an unofficial policy. Or an easy response is to send the proposal back because the proof is insufficient.

One other response for OMB is to seek "outside" help in evaluating regula-tion. An affected industry is always quite willing to supply its data to the White House or to OMB. More and more this is happening. Washington lobbyists now casually ignore agencies and go straight to the White House and OMB. The prob-lem here is that the process becomes highly politicized and data submitted to the White House rarely can be tested in the true light of day. Early in this current administration when I was working on a particular proposal, I was told by OMB that the department's cost figures were inaccurate and the true cost for the pro-posal was 200 million dollars. When I asked for the source of this figure, I was told that it came via a phone call from an industry source. Fearing lawsuit, I requested reconfirmation of the figure, and then was told the industry figure was 100 million dollars. When a formal letter finally came in, the figure was 50 million dollars.

But besides the problems of undue reliance upon cost-benefit analysis and centralization, there is also the problem that the administration has let it be known very definitely that it is opposed to new regulation. It talks of cost-benefit analysis and yet its press releases only refer to costs. Its announcements of cuts in the number of pages in the Federal Register devoted to regulation have a vague resemblance to the body counts of the Vietnam era. Informally, the word is hand-ed down that new regulation need not appear. Confronted with this attitude (and federal bureaucrats are really quite responsive) and the hurdles imposed by OMB, the regulatory process has ground to a virtual halt. When I spoke to people at the various DOT agencies I used to work with, they referred to the regulatory process as dead or a charade. The same is occurring throughout the government.

I would suspect there is much sympathy for such moratorium or impound-ment in this audience. But that may be a short-sighted approach. The current impoundment of the regulatory process, at NHTSA and elsewhere, may very well be an emotional overreaction to perceptions of past excesses, or at least excesses of rhetoric. And the problem with overreactions is that they produce a pendulum that at some point will swing in the opposite direction with equal ferocity. There are still problems, and if one denies their existence, a momentum will build that will deny us the ability to treat these problems in a rational way. Remember now that we have created a regulatory process that is highly centralized and highly politicized. Put that process in the hand of a proregulator, and the result is fairly obvious.

Where the pendulum will swing in the future is a question that is not answerable. It may be towards increased state and local intervention. Let us not forget that much of federal regulation came about in an attempt to curb state regulation. The Motor Vehicle Safety Act preempts local regulation only where NHTSA occupies the field. Many states are now attracted towards local hazardous materials regulations. Conservative Virginia, where I come from, is now considering much more stringent drunk driving laws and a statutory requirement for auto restraints for children. There is considerable sentiment for both these measures. Several other states are moving in the same direction. If they are adopted and don't bring about the hoped-for result, other measures may be sought at the state and federal level. The last round of federal regulation was proceeded by a series of harsh state laws. Four years is not a long time. In fact, two or three years is even a shorter time. I was recently at a law symposium, and a distinguished lawyer made the point that this country's voter is neither conservative or liberal. He or she is a populist with strong feelings against big government but with equally strong feelings against big industry. Which feelings gain prominence is really a question of time.

If subrosa moratoriums are not a solution, or at least not a solution over any extended period of time, what are the alternatives? Emotional responses are not the answer. Nor are partisan ones. There are not easy solutions such as congressional vetos, de novo court reviews, or sunsets. These mechanical attempts at providing solutions simply encourage the Congress to be sloppy in its analysis of new legislation. We have to find some good people to run and staff the agencies. It is at the departmental or agency level that reform can take place. And we have to avoid the creation of adversary relationships on the part of all. This is not a very neat solution, but I fear if we don't proceed somewhat in this manner, we will forever be riding the pendulum of excessive regulation and excessive non-intervention.

Let me end these remarks by quoting from a recent address from Admiral Hyman Rickover to a congressional committee:

> I believe that businessmen must treat government regulation realistically, rather than with instinctive opposition. Much of government regulation is essential to protect the public against the recurrence of past abuses, and because it is unrealistic to expect any group to truly police itself. Businessmen must face the fact that regulation is inevitable. Blind opposition to all regulation detracts from the valid complaints business may have about the excesses of regulation.
> Often the largest businesses—those least subject to the restraints of free enterprise—are the most outspoken advocates of the capitalist, free enterprise system and an effective safeguard against these excesses. They want the public to believe that they behave in accordance with the free enterprise system, when in fact they escape

many restraints of that system. Consistently they lobby against new government regulations. They herald the virtues of competition and the marketplace as if they were small businessmen subject to these forces. Yet at the same time, they lobby for government—that is, taxpayer—assistance in the form of tax loopholes, protected markets, subsidies, guaranteed loans, contract bailouts, and so on.

Businessmen should vigorously advocate respect for law because law is the foundation of our entire society, including business. Few areas of society are as dependent on law as is business. The law protects such essential rights of business as integrity of contracts. When businessmen break the law, ignore or destroy its spirit, or use its absence to justify unethical conduct, they undermine business itself as well as their own welfare.

THE LEGAL FRAMEWORK OF INTERNATIONAL TRADE:
PROBLEMS AND PROSPECTS

Robert E. Hudec

In any discussion of the auto industry's foreign trade problems, one quickly runs into some reference to GATT rules. The remedies provided by U. S. law for injurious import competition, and for dumped or subsidized exports, are all patterned after, and limited by, GATT rules. Proposals for additional limitations on imports are met with reminders that GATT rules may prohibit such action, or at least, may require compensation of some kind. On the other hand, recent investigation of the trade measures employed by other producing countries show that many of these countries are already using measures that seem to violate GATT rules.

The charges and countercharges about GATT violations raise some interesting legal issues for GATT experts. But most people start by asking more basic questions:

What is GATT?
What kind of international law are these GATT rules?
What are the consequences of violating GATT rules?
If GATT rules are so important, how do other governments get away
    with violating them?
Are other governments really playing by the same rules?

As it happens, these questions about GATT law have been a very active topic for the past decade or so, and they are currently the subject of important activity in both Washington and Geneva. GATT is nearing a showdown over an effort to strengthen its rules, and the Congress seems to be moving toward legislation that attempts to force that showdown.

In my remarks today, I would like to address some of these general questions about GATT legal rules. I will say something about what GATT is, and what its rules require. I will then try to give a brief description of how GATT has

Robert E. Hudec is Professor of Law, University of Minnesota Law School.

worked over the past thirty years, what the present reform efforts are about, and where they are likely to lead us.

There are two things my remarks will not do: First, I will not make you sit through a legal analysis of the UAW content bill, the Mexican auto decrees, or any other trade measures. Second, I will not lecture you on the importance of obeying GATT rules. To the contrary, I hope to tell you a good deal about the failings of GATT law, and about the uncertainty that exists today as to whether GATT is a workable legal system any more. This is not a simple issue; it is my hope and belief that education about the complexities is a necessary first step toward rational decision making.

I

What is GATT? The name "GATT" refers to two different things. One is an international agreement titled the General Agreement on Tariffs and Trade. The other is an international organization that takes care of the day-to-day administration called for by the General Agreement. The membership of this organization consists of over eighty governments that have signed the Agreement.

The General Agreement was negotiated in 1947. It is a long and complex document that runs seventy-odd pages of rather small type. The Agreement also contains an appendix, called the Schedule of Concessions, in which all the tariff bindings made by member governments are recorded. In addition to the General Agreement itself, the GATT has created a large body of additional rules and procedures over the past thirty years in the form of side agreements, decisions, and legal rulings. Collected together, all of the legal instruments would fill five or six feet of shelf space.

II

Next, what does GATT say?

Let me speak first in general terms: GATT is not a free trade manifesto. It is a compromise between two conflicting truths that were perceived by the governments in 1947—and are, I think, still perceived today.

The first was the truth learned in the 1930s—that when governments pursue a vigorous policy of trade protectionism, other governments are forced to counter with vigorous protection of their own—with the result that no one gains, and everyone is actually much worse off. Governments had resorted to such policies during the 1930s, and the result had been an unqualified economic disaster. The lesson was clear: Never again.

The second truth was that no government could keep its hands off foreign trade completely. The political system in most western countries made governments responsible for a wide variety of social and economic objectives; government intervention in the economy, including action to protect domestic producers against foreign competition, would sometimes be politically necessary.

The compromise was to write a set of rules that would limit protectionism as much as possible, but with exceptions for those sorts of protective action that governments thought were necessary and legitimate. The Agreement never states a goal of totally free trade. The goal was controlled progress toward greater trade liberalization.

The basic starting point of the GATT rules was a legal model that required all protection to be placed in the tariff, with all forms of nontariff restrictions (such as quotas) being prohibited. Although the Agreement would place no ceiling on tariff rates, the idea was that governments would negotiate reciprocal reductions in their tariffs as they were ready to do so. Whatever the level of the tariff, it was agreed that the rate would be the same for all countries. This was the MFN (most-favored nation) or nondiscrimination principle.

No government was able to promise full compliance with this model. Each major government tacked on exceptions for other kinds of trade barriers it felt it had to have. The list of exceptions was very long. Indeed, exceptions take up much the largest part of the text. GATT's first Director General, Sir Eric Wyndham White, is supposed to have described the General Agreement as "a collection of exceptions, strung together by loopholes."

In 1947, the major exception was the right to use quotas to deal with balance of payments problems. Until the late 1950s, most major GATT members, except the United States and Canada, effectively controlled all imports by the use of such restrictions.

The major long-term exception to the GATT rules was the so-called escape clause, which gave governments the right to impose extra tariffs, or even quotas, on imports that were causing serious injury to a domestic industry. An even broader exception was made for agricultural trade, where the GATT simply accepts the fact that governments will maintain price-support programs, and recognizes that the artificial markets created by these programs will need quotas to protect them against imports. Another exception removed government procurement from all supervision under GATT, so that programs such as Buy-America laws would not be disturbed. And finally, there were wholesale exceptions for trade restrictions based on public policy concerns, such as health, safety, public morals, national security, conservation, and preservation of the national cultural traditions.

A similar series of exceptions was written into the MFN principle. There was an exception for customs unions. There was another exception for the existing preferential tariffs of the major powers—the British Commonwealth preference, the French franc-zone preference, and even some U. S. preferences to Cuba and the Philippines. There was another exception for the European Recovery Program, allowing the countries of Western Europe to give preferential treatment to each other as a way of helping their economies recover from the war.

Finally, there were some special exceptions on behalf of developing countries, granting them the right to use extra protective measures for the purpose of promoting economic development.

On the whole, the compromise stated in the text of the General Agreement was fairly generous, requiring little change in the existing policies of the leading signatories. At the last minute, it was actually decided to write in a general exception for *any* legislation in force in 1947 that did not follow the rules.

Still, the broad prohibitions against nontariff barriers were quite sweeping, and many of the exceptions were carefully limited with long and complex criteria. Judged by prior government practice, GATT was a reasonably demanding set of rules.

III

In actual practice, the GATT rules turned out to be less demanding than the text of the General Agreement seemed to require. In the first place, the rules were never given very clear legal force. In most countries, the GATT was not put into force as a treaty, ratified by legislatures. Instead it was cast as a trade agreement, signed only by the Executive branch. Moreover, it was put into force by an unusual instrument called the Protocol of Provisional Application. To this day, the community of legal experts doesn't really know what "provisional application" means, at least not in any technical legal sense. The term was clearly intended to put some sort of string on the legal commitment; beyond that, it wasn't meant to be clear.

I would stress the fact that the early GATT was never voted on by legislatures. The U. S. Congress went to some lengths to keep its distance. The Congress did appropriate money annually for the U. S. contribution to GATT expenses, but only as part of a general line item for "international conferences" that did not mention GATT by name. The Congress also gave the President authority to negotiate tariff reductions in four different GATT negotiations between 1949 and 1961, but each time the Congress added a proviso expressly stating that its action was not to be construed as approving GATT.

As for the GATT's own legal practice, it developed a rather subtle enforcement procedure. GATT rules were considered private contract rights, not a criminal code. The GATT would never investigate a legal violation unless a member country complained. When a violation was charged, there would first be an effort to settle the matter through bilateral consultations. If that failed, the complaining government could ask for a ruling from the contracting parties. GATT developed a procedure under which a panel of neutral experts would issue objective legal rulings—a sort of in-house arbitration procedure. A ruling that a government had violated GATT would be followed by recommendations and review proceedings, and in most cases these pressures succeeded in producing compliance or, at least, a settlement acceptable to the complaining party. The GATT procedure also provided for the possibility of authorizing trade retaliation. Although retaliation is often threatened, however, it has been used only a few times. For practical purposes, the force behind the GATT legal rules was moral pressure.

The early GATT's performance record was mixed. Tariffs were negotiated downward, and governments did remove their balance-of-payments restrictions, pretty much on time. There were, in addition, a number of important and successful legal proceedings in the first ten years or so.

Over time, however, the GATT began to tolerate a certain number of measures in violation of the rules.

First, no government ever obeyed the agriculture rules in full. In 1955 the United States obtained a total waiver on its agricultural trade restrictions, and then other governments followed similar practices, without legal challenge. Second, the GATT never developed a very satisfactory way of reviewing escape clause actions. Although governments generally exercised restraint in taking such actions, the United States and others never followed the exact criteria of the GATT rule. In recent years, governments have frequently resorted to discriminatory escape clause restrictions, in violation of the MFN rule. Third, on customs unions, although the basic EEC treaty complied reasonably well with the GATT rule, there have been a large number of other customs unions which have not complied, but which GATT has tolerated anyway.

In the case of some rule violations, the affected governments simply did not bring the violations to the GATT's attention, preferring to work things out bilaterally. When nonconforming trade restrictions were brought to the GATT, they were usually accepted informally, without pressing the legal issues to a decision. In some of these cases, the GATT was satisfied that the measures were, on the whole, a reasonable response to a particular problem. But, to be perfectly frank, there were a number of other cases where many GATT members were upset about a nonconforming measure, but simply had to give way to the fact that a government had made up its mind, dug in its heels, and wasn't going to budge for anything short of all-out economic warfare. The GATT community has usually been reluctant to go to war.

There was an even greater retreat on the rules governing developing countries, although most of this was accomplished by negotiated amendments. Developing countries were given still broader freedom to use trade restrictions for balance-of-payments reasons, and to promote economic development. Developing
countries need not give full reciprocity in trade negotiations. Various kinds of
discrimination *in favor of* developing countries are now permitted as exceptions to
the MFN principle. In the recent Tokyo Round negotiations, GATT recognized the
general principle that developing countries are entitled to "special and differential
treatment."

Looking over the record of the GATT for the first twenty-five years or so,
that is up to about 1972, one would have to say that GATT rules had been treated
with a great deal of "flexibility." As more and more rules gave way to pragmatic
settlement, it became harder and harder to say that the rules, in themselves, were
exercising much discipline.

On the other hand, the GATT governments did succeed in establishing a
progressively more liberal trade order during these years. Governments did dis-
mantle the pervasive balance-of-payments controls that were choking world trade
immediately after World War II. They did reduce industrial tariffs, to the point
where, in the view of some observers, they are no longer a significant factor in
international trade. And, although governments erected a significant number of
the new nontariff restraints, the overall flow of trade had increased, and most
observers would have said that world markets were more open than they had ever
been.

The explanation seems to be that, although governments certainly felt free
to bend the rules when it suited their advantage, they were restrained by some
larger sense of not going too far. In part, this restraint arose simply as a matter
of internal economic policy—a policy which usually recognized that protectionism
is costly for the long-term well-being of an economy. In addition, restraint was
also generated by a continued fear of provoking the sort of general trade collapse
that took place when protectionism got out of control in the 1930s. As recently as
the OPEC oil crisis and the mid-1970s world recession, governments found it necessary to convene high-level meetings, outside GATT, to make certain that government reactions to these problems did not trigger a 1930s-type rush to protectionism.

Governments have hardly behaved like choir boys, of course. All governments try to get away with measures that they would not want others to copy, and
sometimes this double-standard approach provokes considerable irritation. Up to
about 1970, however, the main actors seem to have known where to stop.

IV

In the early 1970s, some governments began to express dissatisfaction with this flexible approach to GATT law. It began with a perception that trade barriers were starting to get out of hand. In 1970, the GATT compiled a list of nontariff barriers that had emerged over the last decade—both the various rule violations and also many other trade-restricting practices that weren't covered by GATT rules. The list was quite long, and was getting longer.

In addition, there was a growing concern about reciprocity. It is all well and good to say that governments should sit down and reason together about what trade measures are reasonable in a given set of circumstances, but when there are no preestablished rules by which to measure things, governments inevitably form different perceptions. These differing perceptions led some governments to feel they were not obtaining equal treatment.

The U. S. Congress has persistently questioned whether the United States has been receiving equal reciprocity. In the Trade Expansion Act of 1962, Congress added a new section which urged the President to prosecute illegal or unreasonable trade measures by others, and gave the President power to retaliate, unilaterally, in such cases. In the Trade Act of 1974, the Congress expressed dissatisfaction with the President's very limited use of this authority; so, it expanded the remedy by giving private parties a right to file complaints, and by requiring the President to investigate them. In 1979 the Congress changed the law again to specify more carefully when and how the President must act. And, as most of you know, the Congress is presently considering a number of so-called "reciprocity" bills which are intended to make the President act still more vigorously. That makes four such laws in the last twenty years and *three* in the last *eight* years.

In the early 1970s, these concerns in Washington began to affect U. S. practice in GATT. The United States tried to shake up GATT legal practice by making an inventory of trade complaints and instituting about half a dozen law suits. The United States also took the lead in trying to write new GATT rules, or to rewrite old rules to make them more effective.

All these reform efforts were pressed in the 1973-1979 Multilateral Trade Negotiations, also known as the Tokyo Round. The Tokyo Round produced several new sets of rules and procedures, called "codes," on particular subjects—the main ones being subsidies, dumping, government procurement, product standards, and customs valuation. Governments are currently trying to draft a new escape clause rule called the Safeguards Code. Tighter adjudication procedures were also adopted, although no fundamental change was made in enforcement powers. And, finally, the United States began to try to reverse the growing lack of legal discipline upon developing countries; it secured some measure of acceptance for a "graduation" principle that more advanced developing countries, such as Brazil, must begin to be bound by the same rules that bind the industrialized countries in whose markets they sell.

V

The current situation is that the GATT is just beginning to put the new codes and procedures into operation. In addition, a record number of GATT lawsuits have been filed during the last three years. Close to half the lawsuits have been generated by the United States under its new private-complaints procedure; but many other countries have caught the spirit, including a few who have brought GATT lawsuits against the United States.

It is a bit too early to judge the results. From what little one can see so far, it is clear that a great deal of tension is building. Old habits are far from dead. Many governments are already expressing alarm at possibly overtaxing the GATT's legal machinery, and there is already some resistance to the idea of dealing with trade problems this "legalistic" way.

Looking ahead, one can see that there are a good many obstacles to achieving more effective enforcement. There are still many trade measures in violation of GATT rules. In some cases, the rules themselves probably need renegotiation after thirty years, and that will be difficult. In the case of other violations, governments claim a variety of political and economic difficulties, and it is difficult to know what they can do, or will do. More fundamentally, there is by no means complete agreement over whether, and how strictly, GATT rules ought to be enforced. There is also considerable disagreement about the underlying problem of reciprocity—disagreement not only about whether one country's trade measures are better or worse than another's, but also about whether, and to what extent, countries with lower standards of living owe reciprocity to those which are better off.

The next twelve to eighteen months should give us some indication of where the current pressures for better enforcement will lead. Several significant cases are already before the GATT, and should be decided this summer. Several more are in the pipeline. A ministerial meeting this fall could produce an important reaction, or a counterreaction.

The outcome obviously depends on the actions of the key governments. The first issue will be whether, and how hard, the United States will continue to press for greater enforcement of GATT rules. The United States has been the source of most of the pressure so far, and things will not move forward unless the United States continues.

There are reasons to be skeptical about U. S. intentions. The U. S. Congress has been legislating about reciprocity for twenty years. While the Executive has certainly stepped up the pace of enforcement efforts, it has taken a long time to get this far, and it is still not clear whether the Executive is willing to precipitate a major confrontation over rule enforcement. The United States has many international economic interests that are adverse to any risk of upsetting the status quo, and these interests will be pressing for caution.

The reciprocity legislation currently before the Congress is not critical. The President has all the authority he needs to pursue a vigorous enforcement policy in GATT. In fact, he has had enough authority since at least 1962. The issue is simply the will to use that power, particularly the power to retaliate.

Personally, I think it would be a mistake for other governments to conclude that the United States will not take risks. The Congress has invested a great deal in GATT in recent years. It has changed legislation to conform to GATT, and has legislated about reform of GATT; it now even appropriates money for GATT by name. The Congress is now paying close attention to what happens.

And, whether it is true or not, most of the U. S. officials one talks to these days feel that the United States is not getting the reciprocal benefits it deserves. How many times have you heard it said recently that the United States is the only really open market in the world today? Likewise, the import traumas of recent years, and expecially the problem of auto imports, have persuaded these participants that the United States is no longer a superior economic performer that can afford to take a little less to help out the other guy. And finally, the costs of adjustment to import competition have been rising steadily, making it more and more imperative, politically, to secure equal treatment for our own trade interests. With or without the new reciprocity legislation, these are the elements of a very aggressive policy toward GATT rule enforcement.

The other major factor, of course, will be the response of other countries to all this. I must underline again that there is no easy measure of reciprocity in the world today, and that many other countries are inclined to view U. S. protests about nonreciprocity as self-righteous eyewash. This is a dangerous situation. It will be particularly dangerous if the United States tries to press its claims outside the common legal framework of GATT. Bilateral political approaches, such as the one currently being pursued with Japan, may be productive. But retaliation becomes a nightmare unless the claim is objectively validated under commonly agreed rules, and the retaliation is imposed pursuant to agreed procedures.

If, as I suspect, United States pressure will take the form of more GATT lawsuits, the next issue will be the reaction of the governments being sued. Some of the larger countries may try to block the legal process, something they may have the power to do. At this juncture, that could have very damaging repercussions on U. S. policy. If GATT legal restraints are to retain any meaning, there will have to be some indication that the other side is willing to play by the rules and to abide by the results.

One of the best ways for other governments to contest the U. S. reciprocity claims will be to file countersuits against the United States, concerning the U. S. trade barriers that others believe are equally in violation of GATT. If the United States continues the present pace of its GATT lawsuits, it is virtually certain that a significant number of such countersuits will be filed. Unless the United States is prepared to play by the rules as well, the entire enforcement effort will break down. This is the Achilles heel of the U. S. position.

Clearly, there is a great deal of risk and unpleasantness involved in these enforcement issues. After a time, it is altogether possible that all governments will conclude that trade policy issues are just too complicated to resolve by rules and rule-enforcement, and will decide to return to the ad hoc diplomacy that marked the GATT's middle years. In that event, we shall probably see a continuing rise in protectionism. While I doubt that any sane government is going to allow matters to recede to the chaos of the 1930s, trade policy will gravitate toward lowest common denominators—of which there are, today, many available.

THE INTERNATIONALIZATION OF THE AUTO INDUSTRY:
A JAPANESE PERSPECTIVE

Hideyo Tamura

My subject, "Internationalization of the Auto Industry," is a rather broad subject and could be interpreted in hundreds of ways, but at the suggestion of the Planning Committee I will be submitting my own interpretation of the subject and analysis of what major factors are changing world auto production and trade. Some, or maybe most, of you might not agree with my view, but I understand that the object of this conference is to consider the future of the industry, and my position today is to submit our view of it. I hope it will be of some reference for you to know what a Japanese executive, coming from an auto company, thinks about this subject.

I will deal with the subject from three angles: (1) product development, (2) product sourcing, and (3) product manufacturing. How will changes in the circumstances of these three factors affect the industry and what new systems will be required to cope with the new circumstances?

Product Development

First, the product development side. In the past, each major market used to have its own cars designed by the designing staffs located in that country. For example, cars designed in Australia, for Australians, and by the Australian designers were once regarded as the most desirable. But certain factors are and will be changing this in the future. One factor is the increasing complication of requirements coming from the environmental and marketing side, such as emission standards, safety standards, energy-saving requirements, anti-corrosion requirements, etc. Another factor is the development and incorporation of new technologies, such as new lightweight materials, new electronic devices, computer-aided design

Hideyo Tamura is Managing Director Overseas Operations, Toyota Motor Company.

27

methods, computer–controlled testing programs, etc. To develop a new model under these conditions, huge and expensive facilities are now becoming necessary. Companies need billions of dollars to set up all these facilities and another huge sum of money to operate them. So, for each company it is becoming no longer feasible to have the development facilities scattered at different locations.

On the other hand, the world is getting smaller. Information availability has increased worldwide, and improvements in communication systems make it possible to gather all the necessary information without going to individual locations. Today, with the proper arrangements we can get whatever information we need into one information center: governmental regulations or administrative procedures, road conditions or driving habits, economic situations, etc. So, forced by these requirements and helped by these improvements, current development work will be conducted in a main engineering center as a centralized operation at each company. This centralized operation leads to a new concept of car design. The concept will be to develop one base model for the global market, to develop a model that will comply with major market requirements as they exist, with built-in consideration for adjustments to different requirements.

This new concept and new operation will require new systems. The first is an information–input system. All the regulations and requirements of each major market must be put into one computer memory at the designing center. Thus, the regulations for each country will come to the computer memory and be stored there. A new information–gathering network must be established for this purpose.

The second is an information–output system. All the information thus accumulated in the computer memory must be supplied to the designer at the start of new car design. If one designer, for example, starts to design a bumper, all the requirements and regulations of each market for which the car is aimed must be supplied to him beforehand. Then he can start designing the bumper to comply with all these requirements.

The third system is a testing and checking system. Cars thus designed have to be tested and checked to confirm their compliance with each market's requirements. Simulation tests for different conditions will be necessary, confirmation checks for each standard will be necessary, and systematic programming to execute these procedures will be of vital importance.

These are the systems to carry out global design: the information–input system, the information–output system, and the checking and testing programming. When such systems are established and effectively functioning, cars thus designed and developed at the engineering center will comply with each country's various requirements as a built-in characteristic.

To summarize the first point, increasing complications in requirements forces a centralized, new product-development operation; improvement in world-wide communication favors such direction; and a new concept and system will be required to cope with new circumstances.

Product Sourcing

Second, product sourcing. This new tendency in car development will open ways for multidirectional sourcing of components. In the future, component sourcing will be done on a cross-sourcing basis beyond national boundaries and between car manufacturers, because the concept of the same base model for multiple markets will lead to a "commonization" of parts to used in those markets. It will open ways for parts suppliers to supply the same types of parts for global use. Thus, collective sourcing aimed at a maximum volume effect will be a logical direction in the future, if not at present.

At the same time, geographical distance is now being minimized in the business world by advancement in the communication system. The telefax machine, or rapifax as it is called in some countries, has brought revolutionary improvements in business and engineering communications. With this system, engineers from two countries on opposite sides of the ocean can exchange their drawings and have discussion based on these drawings as if they were sitting on opposite sides of a table. Thus, the distance barrier has disappeared for those who make full use of these technologies and who keep trying to understand each other's language and way of thinking. It is important not only to make full use of the machines, but also to try to understand each other.

Considering this background, although there will be many obstacles which we need time to overcome, the future will increase the possibility of multidirectional sourcing in components and products. This will offer new market possibilities for existing suppliers but, at the same time, will open new competition too. Suppliers with new technology, new ideas, better quality, and favorable cost will capture the market. The important thing is that in order to capture these new possibilities and to exact benefit from them, a new attitude for approaching the market will be required.

I understand that there are many gentlemen from the parts suppliers here today, so allow me to speak in rather straightforward language since we think that is the way to facilitate mutual understanding. In our view, the suppliers who insist on the old-fashioned market approach will be left out of these new possibilities. By the old-fashioned approach I mean that you tell the potential new purchaser: "This is what we have. Are you going to buy or not?" Second, you ask the purchaser to accept the supplier's present quality level, saying that this is our level, and since others are already buying at this level, you should be satisfied. Third, you insist on legal methods to avoid business risk. This involves urging the new purchaser to sign a contract guaranteeing that suppliers will be exempted from any responsibility once the parts are received by the purchaser.

The new attitude for suppliers will be to adjust to the needs of the customers and feel responsible for the products supplied, no matter whether it has been received and no matter whether it is already on the market. The new concept of quality must not rely upon inspection but must be built into the production process itself. That means the producer, not the purchaser, is responsible for the quality. The new concept is also to develop and offer products appealing to the customer. It is not enough to just wait for the request from the customer side, but the supplier should develop new products and offer them to the customer.

Speaking of ourselves, looking into these future possibilities, we started trying to source from overseas suppliers. At present we have thirty such suppliers, and there are already some who have approached us with this new attitude, some offering new products, some offering good service, and some approaching us with nice design, all of which we decided to use. These are encouraging signs, and those who appear in the world market with these approaches will be the ones to grasp the opening possibilities.

To summarize this second point, a new concept in product development will lead to the possibility of multidirectional sourcing. Recent progress in communication devices will offer a favorable background for it, but a new attitude in market approach will be required to benefit from it.

Product Manufacturing

Now to the third point: product manufacturing or, I should say, a marketing and manufacturing point of view.

First, some observations on market trend and customer demand. As was pointed out in Secretary Goldschmidt's report to then-President Carter in 1981, the world market is becoming internationalized, and customers' demands are becoming homogenized. In a sense, customers are moving ahead of manufacturers, setting the groundwork for an internationalized global market. The so-called oil crisis has set the pattern for auto demand, and now the whole world demands small and fuel-efficient cars. Although there might be an argument over the speed and extent of the changes, this tendency basically will not be altered in the future—at least we think not. But within this basic trend, customers are becoming more selective in their actual purchase. Just being small does not sell anymore;

just being fuel efficient does not sell anymore. Customers are buying only those vehicles that appeal to them. That means, within the basic framework of internationalization, customers' tastes are becoming more diversified and versatile. Increasing variety in lifestyles and loosening ties of the community and the family lead to more personalized and individualized demands. Today, peoples' tastes and habits are becoming more easily influenced by other peoples' behavior. Assisted through television networks, fashion spreads from one place to another, changing peoples' likes and dislikes quickly and frequently.

On the other hand, the economic conditions worldwide are becoming more unpredictable. As the national and regional economy is more integrated into the international economy, each nation's economy is becoming more vulnerable to disturbing elements outside its control. The huge oil money moving from one place to another is causing unpredictability in the regional economy. At the same time, political tension in one area affects the economic health of other countries, i.e., what happened in Poland affected the German Mark. Thus, each country's economic situation is becoming more and more difficult to forecast and subject to continuous fluctuations. This is the world in which we live.

Since we are now entering into a new era of uncertainty, a new system of production will be required to adapt ourselves to this new era of uncertainty. What system, then? In the past, a conveyor-line system, one model for one line to pursue maximum efficiency, was regarded as the general, common concept. But recently, demand for each model is always going up and down, with the result that the orders are fluctuating also. In order to minimize damage caused by the fluctuation of demand, a new, more flexible production arrangement to absorb these fluctuations will be required. Each company, within its organization, needs to develop a mixed, flexible production line. One solution will be to put two or three models in one line or to put one model into two or three lines. This will level off the ups and downs of orders on a model-by-model basis.

Between the companies, a new era of competition and cooperation will be required. By competition and cooperation I mean competing with each other on the market side with their final products but cooperating with each other on the production side by utilizing each other's facilities or exchanging components. For example, in Australia, we source pressed panels and castings from General Motors' facilities there, and they in turn will be sourcing aluminum castings from our facilities there when we complete our expansion. Yet the two companies are competing bitterly on the market side with a different final product. That is what I mean by competition and cooperation.

To summarize my third point, the market is becoming international and homogenized; the economy is becoming vulnerable and unpredictable. Therefore, a new production system will be required to cope with this new situation.

Conclusion

In short, the world is changing, the market is becoming international, customers' demands are becoming versatile, and we are entering into a new era of uncertainty. New concepts, new attitudes, and new systems will be required. This new situation will mean new challenge and competition, but it also offers new chances and new opportunities. The world market is open for those who are willing to prepare for it.

It seems that Japanese manufacturers were one step ahead in formulating a new system to exact benefit from these new changes. That, in my view, was our real reason for success in late 1979 to early 1981. But I firmly believe that American manufacturers will be coming up with their own new system in the near future. Already there are signs that they have started to move, and we know from past experience that once Americans start moving, formidable energy will be concentrated in that direction. So, in the not-so-distant future, we will be facing a new challenge from the U. S. side in the global market. Whether you believe it or not, we are expecting that to happen. It will mean new hardship for us, but it will be a good thing for the progress of the industry worldwide, and we think we have to face it.

THE NEED FOR LOCAL-CONTENT LEGISLATION

Douglas A. Fraser

Automotive manufacturing is an industry in crisis: the U. S. car and truck makers have now experienced thirty-seven consecutive months of depressed sales. 1981 sales were down 32 percent from 1978 in cars and 53 percent in trucks. Projected production for the first quarter of 1982 is 37 percent below that of 1981, and 1981 car and truck production was at its lowest since 1952. Yesterday it was announced that during the first ten days in March sales were down again over 30 percent compared to last year, despite the fact that the auto companies are presently giving rebates to customers.

I have read commentators who remark that 1981 was the worst year in the auto industry since 1961, or that January 1982 was the worst January since 1961, but even those comparisons, while they may be statistically correct, considerably understate the case. The population of the United States has grown by 25 percent since 1961. The number of drivers licensed (in other words, the number of potential customers for automobiles) has increased by 75 percent. Sales and production may be at the same levels as 1961, but the market is clearly bleaker now. Perhaps the fact that the number of cars on the road has increased approximately 75 percent since 1961 is the crucial variable.

There are presently in the manufacturing plants at Ford, General Motors, Chrysler, American Motors, and Volkswagen over 250,000 workers laid off indefinitely. This figure does not include those who are being laid off temporarily for a week or so while the auto companies reduce their inventories; nor does it include those tens of thousands who are laid off in the parts supplier industry. At my testimony in Washington before the subcommittee considering proposed local-content legislation on March 3 this year, I heard a representative from the Department of Commerce say, "Well, laid-off auto workers are, after all, protected by Unemployment Compensation and after that by welfare." But I can tell you, we don't want Unemployment Compensation, we want jobs; auto workers don't want welfare, they want to be working.

Douglas A. Fraser is the sixth international president of the United Auto Workers union.

33

The four states of our nation that are most dependent upon the auto industry—Illinois, Indiana, Michigan, and Ohio—are all suffering double-digit unemployment. We've had double-digit unemployment in Michigan now for two long, long years; Michigan unemployment is currently up to a seasonally adjusted rate of 16 percent. In these four states alone, 750,000 workers have exhausted their Unemployment Compensation coverage. If you consider the impact such high levels of unemployment have on social services and programs like Aid to Dependent Children, you have to be deeply concerned.

The depressed condition of the automobile industry also has a direct impact on the federal budget. In 1978, the Big Four, namely Ford, General Motors, Chrysler, and American Motors, made 4.9 billion dollars in profit; in 1980, the same companies lost 4.2 billion dollars. In 1978 those companies paid 2.8 billion dollars in taxes; in 1980 they got *refunds* of 1.8 billion dollars. That's a 4.6 billion dollar net drain on the national treasury, and that doesn't include taxes that unemployed workers weren't paying either.

Moreover, the auto industry isn't just another industry; it is a crucial part of the industrial base of the United States. Automotive manufacturing consumes 21 percent of all the steel used annually in this country; 50 percent of the malleable iron; 34 percent of the zinc; 12 percent of the primary aluminum; 13 percent of the copper; and 60 percent of the synthetic rubber. It is no wonder our layoffs and downturns—to speak plainly, the depression that we're experiencing in the auto industry—have such ripple effects throughout the economy. Some economists estimate that this depression in the auto industry alone has resulted in 1 percent of all U. S. workers being unemployed, and that the cost of that 1 percent (combining the loss to the government of the income taxes that are not paid with the increased cost of social benefits) was 30 billion dollars in 1981.

Now obviously all of these difficulties cannot be attributed to the increase in sales of cars and trucks imported from Japan. Certainly the weakness of the U. S. economy in general must bear the major share of the blame. I would suggest that one aspect of our current economic ill-health is especially noteworthy: the continued high rates of interest.

I've heard it argued that the rates have decreased since the days of the Carter administration. But considering these rates in conjunction with the rate of inflation, real interest rates, the costs of capital, have actually increased. During the Carter presidency, the differential between the prime rate and the rate of inflation was 1 to 3 percent. Today that difference—between 16 percent and 7 percent—is at least three times as large.

Moreover, high interest rates not only make consumers reluctant to buy (and pay high rates on auto loans), but they also have a direct negative impact upon dealerships. Many dealers are small entrepreneurs, with not all that much capital (which is why so many of them these days are going bankrupt). In times of reduced sales, these dealers simply cannot afford to carry large inventories, and they therefore don't order cars from the factories. In addition, to maintain their revenues dealerships must make a profit by margin instead of by volume. For example, rather than making a hundred dollars profit per car and selling three cars, as they might have in yesterday's marketplace, dealers try to make a three-hundred dollar profit on the one car they can sell under current conditions—that's the way many of them are surviving. High interest rates have a more severe impact on the auto industry than on any other sector of the economy besides housing.

Nevertheless, the international trade in cars and trucks, particularly the U. S. trade with Japan, does have some hand in the current U. S. auto industry depression—so much so that I'm willing to call that trade unfair. Between 1978 and 1981, the period I talked about earlier, imports of Japanese cars increased by 37.1 percent and imports of Japanese trucks by 32.7 percent. The U. S. trade deficit with Japan last year, by one measurement, was 16 billion dollars, 13 billion dollars of which was a consequence of the trade deficit in automobiles alone. Calculated over the last five years, the automobile trade between the two countries has resulted in a 47 billion dollar U. S. deficit.

As a result, the UAW is advocating the passage of House Bill 5133—what has been called a local-content bill. We believe that companies should put some capital where their market is; we believe companies from other countries should create jobs where their sales are. After the second World War, when the European market was open to the American auto companies, they didn't export tremendous numbers of cars there. Ford and General Motors built plants in the United Kingdom, France, Germany, Belgium, and later in Spain; Chrysler followed suit. At the same time, U. S. auto companies were shut out of Japan, and couldn't invest or build plants in that country.

The provisions of House Bill 5133 may be briefly sketched. If a company sells between 100,000 and 150,000 vehicles in the United States, they would be required to have a North American content (North American in terms of this legislation means U. S. and Canadian) of 25 percent; companies selling 150,000 to 200,000 cars here would be required to manufacture them with 50 percent North American content; those selling 200,000 to 500,000 cars, with 75 percent; and over half a million cars, 90 percent. All of the U.S. car companies, by the way, have sufficient domestic content to meet these requirements; the domestic content of U. S.-manufactured cars currently runs about 95 percent.

The UAW advocates passage of this legislation despite the various arguments sometimes offered against trade restraint—or against protectionism if you want to characterize our position as protectionistic. But I believe that there is not only moral and ethical justification for content legislation, but economic justification as well. The free trade that protectionism is supposed to endanger is having disastrous economic consequences for the auto industry.

People occasionally accuse me of being a knee-jerk liberal—and occasionally they have a point. I have now discovered that there are also knee-jerk free traders. They are devoted to the principle of free trade regardless of its economic and social consequences. But people in the United States are increasingly beginning to ask the more important question: it may be *free* trade, but is it *fair*? Although the UAW has historically supported free trade, if you ask an unemployed auto worker nowadays "Aren't you for free trade?" he will say "Not when it's killing me." I don't feel that we should sacrifice the auto workers on the altar of free trade when that free trade is not fair trade.

Now it is true that the day I testified, members of the Reagan administration testified against the proposed domestic-content legislation; but even these Republican spokesmen are no longer sounding like free traders. Special Trade Ambassador Brock, Secretary of Commerce Baldridge, and Department of Transportation Secretary Lewis have all complained sharply about our current trade relationship with Japan. Significantly, these three particular men have one interesting thing in common. Before becoming members of the Cabinet, they were businessmen, some of whose dealings were with the Japanese. They can give us chapter and verse on the kind of lopsided, discriminatory trade relationship the United States has had with Japan.

For example, Japan severely restricts the importation of citrus fruits, beef, and tobacco from the United States. Special Trade Ambassador Dave McDonald was in Japan recently, trying to get the restrictions on citrus fruits and tobacco eased. The Japanese government, in typical fashion, established a study committee. The Japanese can be masters of procrastination, and study committees are a fine stalling device. The Toyota Motor Company set up one study committee in 1980, employing a group of researchers from Stanford Research Institute, I think, to advise them whether Toyota should indeed make an investment in the United States—I've heard nothing of it since, although the silence makes me suspicious that I already can guess its findings.

Similarly, in 1980, there was a good deal of publicity attendent upon a parts-buying mission that Japanese automotive manufacturers sent to the United States. Their announced intention was to increase the number of parts purchased from American suppliers. And the outcome of that mission? Well, in 1981, sales of U. S.-manufactured parts to Japanese auto companies increased 4 percent. However, when you take into account the inflation of prices between 1980 and 1981, that actually represents a decrease in the number of parts sold.

Such tactics may be expected as negotiating ploys, and there is evidence the current U. S. administration is less susceptible to them. But U. S. foreign policy has itself done some damage to our automotive industry. For instance, in pursuing a policy of putting economic pressure on the Soviet Union for its interference in Poland, the Reagan administration refused to license the American companies that were going to sell the Soviet Union pipe-laying machinery for constructing a natural gas pipeline from Siberia into West Germany. Disciplining the Soviet Union may be a proper policy, but that particular sanction had more effect on the American workers at the Peoria, Illinois, Caterpillar plant and the Fiat-Allis plant in Springfield, Illinois, then it did on the Russians. The U. S. workers who were going to build the machinery to lay the pipeline lost their jobs. And the Komatsu Company of Japan quickly contracted with the Soviet government to fill the orders for the equipment.

The Japanese themselves have vigorously negotiated local-content clauses in their contracts with American manufacturers, so there is little point to opposing a U. S. local-content law on the grounds of its unfairness. The Japanese contract with Boeing for their next generation of jets, the 767s, calls for 15 percent Japanese content; their agreement to purchase Lockheed Starfighters, 44 percent Japanese content; the McDonnell Douglas F-15s they buy will have 40 percent Japanese content.

Every other country that is a major auto producer has a policy promoting their domestic auto industry and to a degree protecting it. Other governments are often quite aggressive in protecting domestic manufacturers. The United Kingdom secured a quasi-official agreement from the Japanese auto companies to restrict exports into Great Britain from Japan in 1980 to 11.5 percent of that market. The French government has restricted Japanese imports to 3 percent of their market. 1981 was a bad year in the French auto industry—Renault, I see, lost 150 million dollars, Peugeot is not doing too well—so they got the Japanese to agree voluntarily to reduce that 3 percent to 2.5 percent.

Nor is it impossible for an automobile company to trade responsibly and sensitively with the United States. Volkswagen, for years the major importer of cars into this country, now has considerable capital invested here. The company built a plant in Westmoreland, Pennsylvania; before line speeds were reduced, the plant employed about 45,000 American workers. Volkswagen also has a stamping plant in Charleston, West Virginia, and a parts plant in Fort Worth, Texas. The company is renovating a plant in the Detroit suburb of Sterling Heights for another assembly plant, but given the present state of the market, it will probably be delayed.

Now I'm not contending that the only problem for the U. S. auto industry is competition from Japan; the management of domestic car manufacturers has clearly made some mistakes in planning and forecasting in recent years. There is little purpose now in trying to fix the blame. But discussions of current auto industry problems occasionally point a finger at U. S. workers—denigrating their productivity or concern for quality—and those accusations are misplaced. I've heard people say that the workers in the U. S. auto industry are overpaid and lazy. The facts, needless to say, fail to support this canard.

Productivity in the U. S. auto industry is exemplary. It has increased an average of 3.4 percent annually for the last two decades; and this takes into account bad years as well as good. (At present, for example, because of the low volume of production, economies of scale are not working for the industry, and productivity isn't increasing.) The UAW has never resisted new technology and the introduction of productivity-enhancing automation. We realize that if workers are to get a larger slice of the economic pie, we first must bake a larger pie. We understand that increased productivity creates wealth, and accept our responsibility for increasing productivity.

The concessions about which the UAW has been negotiating agreements with domestic auto manufacturers are a telling demonstration of how far workers will go to insure such productivity increases. Although the renegotiated contracts the union has brought to the U. S. automakers are principally designed to protect the job security of its members, it's obvious the wage concessions offered should help the industry meet the Japanese challenge. I must say, however, that the salaries and bonuses of the top U. S. automakers' management are several times larger than those of their counterparts in Japan. The eight-dollar-an-hour wage differential between Japanese auto workers and U. S. auto workers that you hear about doesn't strike most people as dramatic in the context of the hundreds of thousands of dollars' difference between U. S. and Japanese executive bonuses.

Although there certainly is some difference between the average hourly wages of U. S. and Japanese auto workers, it is debatable how large that difference really is. The cost of living in Japan is less than in the United States, and the costs of some particular items in a worker's family budget, like health care, where U. S. costs have been skyrocketing, can be much higher on the average for American workers. At least two dollars an hour of the wage differential ought to be ignored in a U. S.-Japan comparison because the Japanese have a comprehensive national insurance program.

But the higher costs of production are in any case not the only problem U. S. manufacturers face in competing with the Japanese. The fiscal policies of the two governments probably also have an effect, for one thing. For example, of the increase since 1979 in what's called the "landed-cost differential" (the cost to the manufacturer of a car sold in the American market), approximately two-thirds (about one thousand dollars) may be attributable to the Japanese government's policy of undervaluing the yen. This fact has been attracting more attention of late—Special Trade Ambassador Brock, for one, has publicly pointed it out—and it has been common knowledge among banking circles for some time. High interest rates in the United States have their effect here as well.

In addition it is clear that increased consumer concern with quality has adversely affected the competitive position of U. S.-manufactured cars. (The reputation for quality that Japanese cars now carry seems also to be causing

European manufacturers problems, by the way.) One U. S. auto industry mistake has been management's failure to see this interest in quality as a major aspect of marketing. Let me say bluntly that we have not paid as much attention to quality in the auto industry as we should have done. In the industry's flush years, 1977 and 1978, for example, we could sell nearly every car we produced. As a result, because of what some would call the economics of the situation—although greed may be a better word—production *volume* became much more important than *quality*. A plant manager's value to his corporation was judged by whether or not he got his quota of cars out the door on schedule. (Ironically the demand for big cars in those days was quite high, and American small cars as well as Datsuns and Toyotas were selling slowly.)

Well the ball game has changed now. Both auto industry management and our workers have become aware that the quality of our product must improve. Sensitivity to quality has greatly increased, and we've seen distinct improvements in this area over the last eighteen months at least.   Another point worth mentioning here is that product safety ought to be understood as an important aspect of quality. And it has been often demonstrated that most American cars are safer than Japanese cars. Certainly that U. S.-produced cars may protect their occupants better in an accident is no excuse for their having door handles that fall off. Those kinds of quality problems are receiving increased attention. But we can be proud of building, engineering, and designing cars that are safer for the consumers who purchase those cars. As for the problem of absenteeism, which also adversely affects product quality, it seems to be a problem in the labor market of every nation except Japan—and it isn't restricted to industrial workers either.   But the Japanese demonstrate that there may be ways of solving the problem that we haven't sufficiently pursued.

Let me conclude by saying that the U. S. auto industry is indeed in a desperate situation. Through the new agreements we've sought with U. S. manufacturers, auto industry workers have taken steps to fulfill our responsibility for pulling ourselves through this crisis. And by assuring auto workers improved job security, the innovative agreements we're reaching should be a fitting reward for accepting such responsibilities. Clearly the sense of shared pride and responsibility found among Japanese auto industry labor and management may be something worth emulating. Moreover, it is our hope that the Congress of the United States will, by enacting local-content legislation, give our workers and companies some of the kind of protection that the Japanese give theirs. Thank you very much.

RESPONSES OF CONFERENCE PANELISTS
TO AUDIENCE QUESTIONS

Panelists in the morning question and answer session were Mark G. ARON, Assistant General Counsel, CSX Corporation; Robert E. HUDEC, Professor of Law, University of Minnesota Law School; Lee PRICE, Research Department, UAW; and Hideyo TAMURA, Managing Director of Overseas Operations, the Toyota Motor Company. Moderator for the discussion was Paul W. McCRACKEN, Edmund Ezra Day Distinguished University Professor of Business Administration, The University of Michigan.

Q: Would you comment on the proposed relaxation of clean air standards? If there are still problems, how should they be handled?

ARON: I'm stretching my expertise to comment about the National Highway Traffic Safety Administration (NHTSA), and can't offer anything specific about clean air. But in general I don't see great benefits in the centralized bureaucracy that is in place now. The reviewers and planners in the OMB (Office of Management and Budget) are too few and too far removed from the process to have a good firm grasp on what's going on.

I think the focus for reform has to lie within the agency itself. There are plenty of review mechanisms already in place; what exists is a professional bureaucracy reviewed by a political appointee at the agency level. The programs such agencies administer undergo review by another professional bureaucracy and then ultimately by a Cabinet secretary. There's plenty of review there, and those people, I think, are close enough to the situation to make some reasonable compromises between safety and cost.

Q: Regarding the distinction made by Mr. Fraser between free trade and fair trade, how fair is it to impose a de facto tax on American consumers by forbidding us to buy superior Japanese products at significantly lower prices than the less well-designed and built products of U. S. manufacturers? Why don't we begin to compete on quality and price and concern for customers?

PRICE: I'm not sure I could be more persuasive than Doug Fraser on anything, but I would like to reaffirm one point he made: we are concerned about quality. There has been a problem with quality, and we have been trying to deal with it. As for forbidding American consumers from buying what they want, that's simply not our proposal. We would like the American consumer to continue to have the same variety of choice in buying products. We think our proposed local-content legislation can achieve that.

We respect the effects of competition on improving production—in quality, in equipment, and in design. All we are suggesting is that companies that market here, produce here. This need not restrict the choices of the American consumer, nor need it result in any major increase in the price of U. S.-manufactured automotive products. Various kinds of political decisions can affect prices; one that seems to be doing so at the present is the undervaluation of the Japanese yen. Three years ago the value of the yen relative to the dollar was something around 30 percent higher—and at that point the costs of production for Japanese and U. S. automotive manufacturers were comparable. There is reason to believe that revaluation of the yen would restore some of that comparability today. Producing Japanese-designed cars in the United States, in any case, need not make U. S. designed cars cost any more than they do otherwise.

Q: How would a local-content bill of the sort proposed by Mr. Fraser accord with GATT (the General Agreement on Trade and Tariffs)? Do many other countries have comparable bills?

HUDEC: The answer to the first question is relatively simple: the proposed legislation, depending on how it is structured, would be a violation of the GATT. The way that HR 5133 reads now, it would require the imposition of quotas if a manufacturer did not meet the local-content requirements. The quotas would, in the year following, limit the imports of such a manufacturer to 75 percent, I think, of the previous year's sales. Using such quotas is a violation of the GATT.

There is a second legal problem with the proposed local-content bill, which is that it defines domestic content to include both the United States and Canada. This discriminatory treatment in favor of Canada would violate the MFN (most-favored nation) clause of the GATT. However, so does the present agreement that we have concerning duty remission on Canadian products. This was the subject of a GATT waiver granted back in the 1960s, on the theory that it wasn't really harming other nations, and was a rational way of dealing what is in some sense a unitary industry. I doubt that the larger discriminatory aspects of the local-content bill would be granted a waiver today.

As to the second question: Yes, other governments do have domestic-content requirements in force. I think that the ones whose requirements, through quotas or other means, are openly established do violate the GATT. One difficulty here in regard to the policies of some other countries is that often these content arrangements are made between the government and the manufacturer, and are not codified as law. Frankly, this is a very difficult problem. The administration is now trying is to get a handle on this; it may be a situation in which some negotiations leading to new rules would be a necessary first step.

Q: Do you mean that if, for example, a country's government agreed that Toyota could have a certain portion of its domestic market, providing they met certain conditions—but that this did not involve an agreement between the U. S. government and the Japanese government—then it would fall outside the GATT framework?

HUDEC: The GATT deals specifically with governmental actions: laws, rules, and regulations. It would be difficult, for instance, to decide whether the GATT covers something like a deal between the Canadian government (under its foreign investment review policy) and a manufacturer, where the issue is whether or not the government will allow an investment or an expansion of one. I suppose if you could prove a government imposed requirements as a condition of the company's doing business there, you would have a GATT violation. The difficulty in that case is getting the company on the stand; once a company has made such a deal, it doesn't particularly want to disturb it.

Q: Would the Japanese accept a local-content bill requirement along the lines that Mr. Fraser indicated as a fair trade method? If not, why not?

TAMURA: I don't want to start arguing with the UAW now. But I have a high respect for the American people; I believe them to be outgoing, positive and full of challenging spirit. I don't think that Americans will retire to the bedroom just because it's become a bit chilly outside now. That is all I have to say.

Q: Mr. Aron expressed the opinion that governmental regulation ought to settle at some "saturation level," which could then be subject to year-to-year adjustments. But how, once the regulative bureaucracy is in place, is it to be controlled? Won't the bureaucrats' self-interest dictate their activity, and lead them to act to protect their positions and expand their powers?

ARON: I think it's a misconception that regulation springs from an entrenched bureaucracy. Bureaucrats are really quite responsive to the political leadership. Congress establishes regulatory statutes; the President appoints administrators, who act on established policies. It is noteworthy that the same people who were at NHTSA in the early 1970s are at NHTSA today. The people who earlier acted to set up the regulatory structures demanded by Congress and the Executive branch are now acting to rescind them. The easiest answer is to make sure that the people in charge of a government bureaucracy are politically sensitive.

Q: Is it true that UAW workers in the Big Three earn wages and fringe benefits totalling 150 percent of the average for U.S. industrial workers? Is there any justification for this margin?

PRICE: I've seen various estimates comparing the total compensation received by auto workers and by other manufacturing workers. All of them show that auto workers are paid more—some estimates say more than 50 percent more, some say not that much. Auto workers in every country with a major auto industry are paid substantially more than the average manufacturing wage. In part, this difference results from the type of work done in an auto plant; but more importantly it reflects the high productivity of auto manufacturing. The record of the U.S. auto industry over the last thirty years demonstrates this. The industry ranks right at the top in profitability and improving productivity. So that in terms of unit labor costs—which is the crucial measure here, not hourly costs—unit labor costs in the U.S. auto industry have not risen more than the national average during this period. As our latest bargaining with the industry has shown, we take account of economic realities as each new round of contract bargaining occurs. Certainly auto workers are paid more, and we think it's clear that responsible collective bargaining has played the major part in attaining that result.

Q: Judging from its response to the proposed domestic-content bill, the U.S. Congress seems to give little consideration to GATT or other international trade rules. Are we certain to follow a mistaken trade policy? Don't the U.S. trade acts of 1974 and 1979 establish sufficient trade procedures?

HUDEC: There's an interesting conflict between the proposed content legislation—I believe HR 5133 has over a hundred sponsors in the House of Representatives—and the reciprocity bills, which are moving forward in both the Senate and the House, sponsored by the chairmen of the trade subcommittees. It is said that the reciprocity bills have a decent chance of passage this year, but the content bill probably doesn't. These proposals are pushing us in different directions.

The reciprocity bills call for us to enforce more aggressively the GATT rules and trade agreement rights; the content bill would permit us to take actions that would violate those rules. Tension of this sort is a constant in trade policy making. I don't think you can characterize Congress as a whole as being behind either one of these bills. It is interesting, however, that Congress has been giving considerable attention to GATT—first during the Tokyo Round negotiations, second in the 1979 act which ratified the results of those negotiations, and third in the support now found for reciprocity legislation.

I don't believe our trade policy is necessarily mistaken. The problem in trade policy making is to explain it to citizens adversely affected by it. If other countries in the world are pursuing more protectionist policies, then the political difficulty of explaining our relatively more liberal trade policy is greater. Reciprocity's principal importance may be its effect on *national* and not *international* politics.

Are the U. S. trade acts of 1974 and 1979 enough? I think they are. I don't believe the reciprocity bills will significantly affect the legal questions involved in U. S. international trade. The bills are a statement of political dissatisfaction with the way the executive currently pushes U. S. trade rights.

PRICE: I have several comments on these trade issues. One is that the UAW represents not only auto workers but also workers in the construction equipment industry, the aerospace industry, and the farm equipment industry—all of which export between 25 and 50 percent of their production. Caterpillar exports almost 60 percent of its production. We are concerned about U. S. trade policy in a number of industries.

In the second place, the countries that have taken trade measures to ensure stable production levels in their manufacturing industries include many of the most important industrialized countries in the world. France, Britain, West Germany, Belgium, Spain, and Australia have all taken measures far more "protectionist" than the United States has. Japan itself has done a great deal to ensure that domestic production in most industries keeps pace with domestic sales. The rate of unemployment there runs about 2 percent. The Japanese are having what we would consider minor problems in some of their industries—aluminum, steel, and textiles; they are taking measures to ensure that imports don't erode domestic production and cause substantial dislocation. In contrast, the U. S. government did little to support the domestic auto industry between 1978 (when the Japanese manufacturers' share of our market was 12 percent) and 1980 (when it had risen to 22 percent).

A third point is that some sort of Safeguard Code to require international trade agreements to be open and public seems to be necessary. The British instituted restrictions on Japanese auto manufacturers' imports in 1975 and the French instituted very stiff ones in 1978 that weren't known about in the United States until some time later.

Q: Mixed-model assembly has created serious quality and inventory problems for U. S. car manufacturers. What are the Japanese plans and procedures for employee training in inventory control?

TAMURA: The new mixed-model assembly lines require new systems to orchestrate stock control and parts supply; synchronizing these new production systems means synchronizing all their parts, and that can be a very complicated problem if it's handled by stockpiling components in the top floor of the factory.

We decided to give much of the responsibility for coordinating and adjusting the new system to the manufacturing work force on the shop floor. They needed training to do so, which normally required about three or four years in our experience. Some idea of the procedures the Japanese auto companies followed can be found if you study our Just-in-Time systems, to be discussed at the workshop session of this conference.

Q: What role has the insurance industry played in the issuance of NHTSA regulations? Most of the benefits of such safety measures as impact resistant bumpers accrue not to consumers but to insurance carriers. Did the Department of Transportation recognize this and act effectively in this area?

ARON: It seems to me that the insurance companies acted in the matter of auto safety standards like any other well-organized, effective and aggressive interest group—they promoted their own self-interest. Sometimes such lobbying results in good things—the industry was responsible for supplying much detailed information on auto safety that the Department of Transportation used in evaluating the effectiveness of some of its regulations. But the insurance industry can probably be held responsible for the car bumper standards, which are no longer really safety standards. These have far more to do with what's called a car's "crashability"—although I think "repairability" would be a better term—than with occupant safety. NHTSA ran into problems whenever it issued regulations outside the safety area—it is arguable that fuel economy standards may have had certain adverse effects on auto safety.

I believe that market solutions are usually the best in these situations, but it seems clear that we may have missed the boat by trying to depend on the insurance industry to achieve some of these auto safety standards.

Q: How should fairness in international trade be defined? Are the Japanese playing fair?

HUDEC: "Fair" is a political word, and to the extent that it has meaning in international law, it corresponds to the political policies various countries pursue--such as whether there is roughly the same degree of protectionism in their foreign trade policies or whether they offer similar market opportunities to foreign manufacturers. It is almost impossible to conduct rational discussions of fairness in foreign trade without some basic rules that define what is expected in various circumstances. For example, we have heard about several things Japan has done to limit imports in various areas. If these are contrasted with U. S. trade policies, it will immediately become clear that trade restrictions are not always comparable. The U. S. would argue that our controls on imports of television sets was justified by the GATT escape clause because our industry was being seriously injured but that similar Japanese restrictions in other areas can't be compared with ours because ours was justified and theirs weren't. Without some kind of common rule there's no way to judge whether or not countries are following equivalent policies of trade regulation.

Q: Honda of America has announced that it will build a U. S. auto plant which will produce products with a 40 to 50 percent U. S. content. This will provide jobs in the United States, but will not support the U. S. industry—it could even increase competitive pressures on domestic manufacturers. What does the UAW think about such a plan?

PRICE: The UAW has contended that all foreign auto companies with large volume sales in the United States should have major production facilities here. We know quite well that that doesn't necessarily improve the situation for U. S. companies. We advocate this because we want a viable auto industry in this country. Both Honda and Nissan (which is building a truck plant here) intend to have some modest content of parts purchased in the United States, which will help out some suppliers. If we can get the kind of investment we are seeking legislation to assure, such investment by foreign manufacturers will help out even more. It need not increase the competitiveness of General Motors' assembly, but it will assist the basic auto industry.

In January 1982 the utilization of production capacity in the auto industry was 43.6 percent; that's the lowest rate ever recorded by the Federal Reserve Board in over three decades of capacity utilization reporting. The idling of that much equipment and labor has tremendous costs for the entire industry, including suppliers. So it does help General Motors to compete if its suppliers are producing at higher capacity (and therefore lower cost). Another way foreign auto makers' investment here helps the U. S. economy is that it reduces the volatility of changes in the business climate. A more diversified domestic auto industry, as Mr. Tamura reminded us, can adapt more readily to market changes; the industry, and its workers in particular, will not be so vulnerable to the kind of violent swings we've had in the past.

It seems to me that trade reciprocity should be defined in terms of the entire economic relationship between countries—including service and technological exchange as well as capital investment. In these terms, the United States is definitely getting the short end of the stick in our relations with Japan. Since Japan has a very high rate of savings relative to domestic investment, more capital expenditure by Japanese companies with access to that savings would make for a more equitable reciprocal economic relationship.

Q: While Honda and Nissan are building assembly plants in the United States and planning to increase their local purchases of parts, why is Toyota so reluctant to make similar moves?

TAMURA: I understand that the object of this conference is to discuss the future of the auto industry in general, not to deal with individual companies' business activities. So I will refrain from commenting on what Honda or Nissan is doing. But if we are to start some operation, it should be such an operation that will contribute substantially to solving industry's problems and at the same time would not damage our ability to supply products of excellent quality to our customers—which is the principal source of our business strength. When we succeed in forming up feasible ways to carry out these objectives, we will be doing it. It's worth pointing out that Toyota does have a small plant in Los Angeles, although admittedly it doesn't contribute substantially to solving the problems of the U. S. auto industry.

Q: What is the relevance to the "escape clause" of the GATT to the problems we are discussing this morning?

HUDEC: The decision of the U. S. International Trade Commission (ITC), by a three-to-two vote, that the problems of the U. S. auto industry did not qualify under the escape clause test because increased imports were not the principal cause of the industry's difficulties came as a surprise to many people. Three of the ITC commissioners thought that the general downturn of the U. S. economy was a more serious cause than the increased penetration of imports into our market. The two dissenting commissioners didn't disagree with that judgment; they felt that the statute should not be read to cumulate the various factors leading to the economic downturn, but rather, that each factor, such as high interest rates, should be weighed against increased imports.

The reaction of the U. S. Congress was, I think, significant; if Japan had not agreed to restrain exports voluntarily, a quota bill would have been passed. Congress was, in effect, going to overrule the ITC's judgment. I think the reaction of the Japanese government and the Japanese auto manufacturers was as much as to say that some restraint *was* justified. I did not detect any interest in making an international fight over whether the United States was justified in imposing quotas or in asking for voluntary restraints. The decision was a close one, so I don't think the statute needs to be amended, since it could easily have been interpreted the other way, and probably will be the next time.

Q: Why hasn't NHTSA addressed the most significant factor in auto safety, namely the drivers? If consumers *used* the safety equipment already included in their vehicles, the reduction in auto-related injuries would outstrip all gains to date. It seems futile to pass additional legislation and impose further regulations when consumers don't cooperate in the safety effort.

ARON: Making consumers use safety equipment is a problem. Other countries have in fact decided that the course to follow is to pass laws requiring that people "buckle up." Some studies have shown these types of statutes to be effective, because citizens elsewhere may be more law-abiding or more fearful of authorities, or for other reasons. But it is believed by many that such legislation couldn't be enacted in the United States, and if enacted couldn't be enforced. Because the current administration is reluctant to introduce new regulation, there are campaigns underway to solve the problem by educating the public. I'm not sure that the auto industry would want to support this approach, since the scare tactics necessary to get the public to move are often quite gruesome. These may unfortunately lead people to question whether they want to do so much driving.

Q: To follow up on this point: you identify two problems here. One, could such legislation be passed? And two, what would be the incidence of compliance with it if it was?

ARON: I think enforcing compliance would be very difficult, although in specific cases not impossible. Child restraint legislation has been proposed in Virginia and several other states. These require that children under a certain age must ride in "love seats," and I think these would be enforced by prosecuting anyone in an accident involving unprotected children. It is not that difficult to determine if a car had a "love seat" or not. Passage of this kind of legislation depends greatly on its acceptance by the public, and for some reason fairly harsh measures seem acceptable in the child safety area. Similar methods of enforcing a buckle-up law would be less effective, since determining after an accident whether the occupants of the automobile involved were using seat belts at the time would be difficult.

Q: In the light of currently falling oil prices, is it likely that consumers may again demand bigger cars? How could auto makers respond to that?

PRICE: I think we may already be seeing increased demand for relatively larger cars, but I don't anticipate any sudden or dramatic shifts in that direction. Consumers are sensitive to the relative costs of owning a larger car, balancing them against performance criteria. The price of gasoline is a major difference in the costs of operating cars of various sizes. I don't believe that the 1979 shift in consumer preference to smaller cars will be reversed. At the same time, the improved fuel efficiency of the larger U. S. automobiles may, given the current gasoline prices, make them more accessible to a bigger domestic market.

But product quality will also continue to play an important part in the American consumer's choice of automobile, also balancing concerns about fuel economy. In this context I would like to respond to Mr. Tamura's remark earlier that Toyota was reluctant to invest in manufacturing facilities in the United States for fears that it could not maintain product quality. Toyota is producing automobiles in countries other than Japan—in Australia, for instance—and is negotiating to establish production facilities in Brazil and Spain. I've never seen a study of the quality of workmanship in these countries that shows them superior to American workmanship. Spokesmen for both Volkswagen and Honda have testified that the quality of workmanship in their U. S. plants is superior to that in their companies' domestic plants.

TAMURA: The question here is whether there will be an increase in demand for bigger cars and if so, how the auto companies might react to it. Every product planner in the industry is concerned about how market demands will change. We don't pretend to be wise enough to predict how consumers will behave, but it seems to us that the basic trend toward smaller cars will not be changed. How would Toyota react if it does? Our company has no intention of covering the whole U. S. market. We will keep supplying small cars for those people who want them.

Q: In a fully competitive consumer-oriented economic system, shouldn't customers have the option to buy or not to buy features now covered by regulation? Wouldn't consumer demand compel some or all manufacturers to provide such features as options?

ARON: The short answer is yes, but with certain exceptions. I think we ought to rely upon market mechanisms to supply consumers with most of the things they want. But philosophical problems arise in the consideration of unusual cases, like whether people who wanted to ride motorcycles should be required to wear crash helmets. In other cases, market mechanisms may inadequately protect the public. I may want a cheap set of brakes on my car or an inferior headlight system or whatever because of my present economic status, but unfortunately my decision affects other people's lives. These are legitimate areas for government intervention. One often hears that safety simply doesn't sell in the United States; so without government regulation a safety-conscious consumer may be confronted with choices that are too limited.

Q: Aren't claims that auto workers are extremely productive belied by two facts: that most productivity improvements result from capital investment, and that other workers have improved their productivity also?

PRICE: We don't claim that auto workers' moving faster and faster on the production line, like Charlie Chaplin in *Modern Times*, accounts for the productivity improvement in the auto industry. It's obvious that productivity improvement comes by and large through the improvement of the capital equipment that our members work with. That we readily acknowledge. Our point is that, in contrast to other unions in other periods, in other countries, and in other industries, the UAW has been outspoken in favor of productivity improvement. We have recognized that it benefits us as well as the consumer, and for that reason it's been easier for the auto industry to implement improvements in productivity.

On the other hand, there are opportunities for the labor force to improve productivity irrespective of capital investment. The UAW has been very interested in improving the training available to our members, for one thing. The recent Ford contract gives us additional opportunities through our involvement with the company to encourage workers in the plants to do more, and more sophisticated, work. We realize that in the long run there's a trade-off between the loss of jobs as a result of increased productivity and the loss of jobs from losing competitiveness by not having increased productivity.

NOTES ON A TRIP TO JAPAN:
CONCEPTS AND INTERPRETATIONS

William J. Abernathy
Kim B. Clark

The success of Japanese companies in visible and important U. S. markets has created a growth industry among academics: studying and explaining the Japanese approach. Travellers to Japan return with tales of wondrous feats, mysterious organizational landscapes, marvelous new machines, and strange but effective customs and practices. It is difficult to read an article on Japan's success without hearing about harmony, bottom-up management, robots, a docile union, lifetime employment, and a government friendly to business.

The importance of product quality and high productivity to Japan's economic success became especially apparent to us in our study of the U. S. auto industry in the late 1970s. As we examined the possible sources of Japan's competitive advantage, it became clear to us that the notions then popular (more advanced automation, robots) were only part of the story. We found that managerial practices and systems were also a major factor and that many of these (e.g., the Just-in-Time inventory system) were quite distinctive. Did the Japanese auto producers learn these skills, as some experts claimed, from U. S. consultants and companies? After trying to sort through the written evidence, we became convinced that we needed to see the Japanese production process first hand. And so, like many others, we succumbed to the lure of the East and set out for Japan. Our visit encompassed three weeks of intensive exposure to the world of the Japanese auto industry. We visited all the major producers, studied twenty-five plants, and engaged in numerous discussions with senior executives, production and marketing managers, foremen, lineworkers, staff specialists, consultants, academics, and government officials. Our previous field research in the U. S. industry and in Europe proved invaluable in casting the Japanese experience in a comparative context.

William J. Abernathy is Professor and Kim B. Clark is Assistant Professor at the Graduate School of Business Administration, Harvard University.

This report of our visit is both an account of what we saw and heard and a systematic interpretation of our observations. We compare the Japanese plants we saw to their U. S. and European counterparts, and we argue that the methods used by Japanese auto producers can be usefully seen as an extension of the approach to production developed by Henry Ford in the years before the first World War, but seemingly disregarded in the prosperity of the postwar era. In one important respect—the integration of workers into the production system—we find that Japanese practice differs markedly from the American early and late. To this difference in work force management we pay particular attention.

> If Henry Ford were alive today I am positive he would
> have done what we did with our Toyota production system.
> —Taiichi Ohno, Toyota Motor Company

Mr. Ohno, principal architect of Toyota's production system, here raises a fundamental question about the origins of the production methods found in the Japanese auto industry. Is the spectacular progress in productivity and competitive effectiveness that that industry has made based on the refinement of concepts and practices or, alternatively, is it based on a substantial breakthrough in either or both? The principles of Japanese management—among them, lifetime employment, Just-in-Time inventory systems, quality circles, and the zero defect approach to quality—are now legendary in the United States and in other Western countries. Typically, however, Western writers view them as Japanese creations, not as extensions of prior concepts. Further, to the extent those writers treat Japanese management as a cluster of independent policy options, they pay little, if any, attention to the interaction of such policies in their effect on the production process.

Understanding the elements of the Japanese approach, their roots, and their interaction was the main objective of our three-week-long visit to the Japanese auto industry. Our research prior to the visit had revealed that Japanese producers enjoyed a sizable cost and quality advantage. We had toured a variety of automotive facilities in the United States and Europe and thus were prepared to place our observations in Japan in a comparative context. The question we wanted to ask was simple: What explains the Japanese advantage? What is really different about what Japanese managers do? How is this applicable to U. S. management? And how much of Japanese practice can be applied piecemeal or to what extent must the system be adopted in total?

I. Plant Visits and Discussions: Food for Thought

Our visit began with a very hospitable reception at Tōyō Kōgyō's main offices in Hiroshima. This was no ivory tower headquarters: the main offices occupied a corner of the company's large multiplant production complex at the mouth of the Enko River. Tōyō Kōgyō, producer of Mazda cars and trucks, was a good place to start. Long a technical leader in the Japanese industry (it was the first company to employ robots, the first to apply computer-controlled assembly, and the first to massproduce the rotary engine), Tōyō Kōgyō had come close to bankruptcy in the mid-1970s. Its remarkable turnaround centered on dramatic improvements in productivity, and the changes made in its production system were still fresh in the memories of participants.

Problems began with the 1973 oil crisis. The famous rotary engine, which Tōyō Kōgyō pioneered, became an albatross when it received a very low U. S. government EPA fuel economy rating in 1974. Sales of the very popular engine plummeted in the U. S. market, and management at Tōyō Kōgyō faced a real dilemma. Thousands of workers and billions of yen worth of new capacity had been added in anticipation of a strong demand for rotary-powered vehicles. But as sales declined, profits before adjustments dropped from a 12.8 billion yen high in 1973 to a loss of 17.3 billion yen in 1975. Management had simultaneously to make adjustments in the work force, cut inventories, reposition its product, and rapidly achieve efficiency goals.

In a bold move that would be unthinkable in a U. S. firm, excess factory workers were mobilized as salesmen and sent into the field to "sell themselves back to work in the factory." Management introduced a stringent cost-control program and launched a full-scale production rationalization program. The results were striking. Productivity rose dramatically, and work-in-progress inventory was reduced systematically from a seven-day level in April of 1975 to a two- or three-day level in 1981. The number of labor hours per vehicle produced also dropped dramatically over this period—from 96.9 hours per car in 1974 to 66 in 1977, a 30 percent cut in labor content in just two years. (The degree of vertical integration remained substantially unchanged during this period. Productivity estimates are based upon an assumed 1850 hours per year per employee. Comparable rates for other years are: 1973, 91.4; 1974, 96.9; 1975, 91.9; and 1976, 79.4.)

What produced this dramatic improvement? Our interviews with the managers involved focused on new concepts in production, the commitment of employees, and a change in management personnel and style. The new concepts in production were variants of the approach developed by Ohno and his colleagues at Toyota. A project manager in the production planning group described the philosophy behind the new approach:

The New Production System, which is the company's goal, is a system
designed to provide "what is needed by the customer at a reasonable
price at the highest level of quality within the shortest possible period
of time." The ideal form of the new system is analogous to a water
pipeline through which water flows smoothly. In the actual production lines, this translates to the elimination of floats, enabling a synchronized production at a given cycle time.

Realization of a tightly coordinated and synchronized flow of production
required substantial changes in set-up times, enhanced methods to allow workers
to handle more operations, and improved quality. Indeed, improved quality was a
theme we heard again and again.

The quality approach at Tōyō Kōgyō emphasized total quality in all aspects
of value delivered to the customer. An emphsis on quality extended from the
president of the company down to the newest recruit. Some 15,000 employees
participated in Mazda Quality Circles (MQ), the company name for quality circles. The 1,900 circles at Mazda tend to concentrate on improvements in both
production process and quality of the product. In 1980 MQ circles, together with
other recommendations, yielded 900,000 suggestions, 60 percent of which were
implemented. Since this means almost one recommendation per week per employee at Tōyō Kōgyō, we had difficulty in understanding what this number really
meant. How could such a large number be evaluated or implemented? While
many of the suggestions may have been relatively trivial, a significant fraction
dealt with substantive changes in operations. The managers we interviewed
stressed the importance of "bottom-up" management and employee commitment
in the firm's turnaround.

Into the Plants

It was a short ride from the headquarters building to the plants. For the
proverbial John Doe, walking into a Japanese automobile plant cannot be very high
on the list of "sights to see in Japan." But for us, familiar with reports of productive efficiency, there was a definite sense of anticipation and even excitement.
Yet our strongest reaction as we made our way through engine, stamping, and
assembly plants was an impression of "sameness." In important aspects these
plants were just like their counterparts in Detroit, Wolfsburg, or Paris.

It may have been newspaper stories about robots running factories without
workers or the mystery of the kanji characters or the shock of being unable to
decipher street signs or what we already knew about labor productivity in
Japanese plants, but we expected something exotic. Yet there were the same
tunnel broaches, boring machines, transfer lines, welding guns, giant sheet-metal
presses, and clanking assembly lines, drawing jobs by each worker at just about the

speed that Henry Ford first set in 1914. The mystery of the East evaporated in front of our eyes; each machine was a clone of some device in the West. We were in an *Automobile Plant*. Yet, our sense of "sameness" was to prove but a backdrop for the very significant differences that would emerge on a deeper reading as the trip continued.

As we proceeded through the facilities at Tōyō Kōgyō, it seemed as though we brought bad luck! Transfer lines began to shut down, and alarms flashed after us. (Was this for our benefit?) With this turn of fate, however, some important differences between Japanese and U. S. plants began to emerge. When viewing similar line failures in a U. S. plant, one would expect to see the operator stand by and await the arrival of the repairman, the foreman, and perhaps a skilled crafts-man, who would then no doubt discuss whether it was the electrician or the mechanic who had jurisdiction for repair. Employment contracts restrict the kinds of things (maintenance, repair, etc.) an operator could do. In Tōyō Kōgyō, however, the operator and foreman seemed more like players on a seasoned base-ball team successfully executing a triple play. The operator began to diagnose and repair his own machine with the active assistance of the foreman while nearby workers aided in clearing the line of clogged work in process. The teamwork brought the line back into operation shortly. As it turned out, transfer lines at Tōyō Kōgyō were down for repair only 3.9 percent of the time in 1981, and the car body welding line only 1.4 percent of the time. U. S. experience is typically many times higher. We found differences in uptime to be a major factor in explaining the Japanese edge in productivity.

This same spirited teamwork was also evident in the process of changing the dies on the giant presses used in forming sheet-metal body parts. Whereas the experience in U. S. stamping plants is for die changes to take several hours at a minimum, at Tōyō Kōgyō—with the quick-change die arrangement—it only took around five minutes. The technological capability for quick-change dies is avail-able to U. S. producers, but because of industry structure they have been under less pressure to avail themselves of it. When viewed in perspective, it is clear that these dramatic differences in set-up times stem from differences in philos-ophy about inventory policy. In the United States, where set-up times are taken as a constraint and inventory is used to buffer operations, the process has been optimized around these givens. This has led, over time, to the centralization of stamping plants so that high set-up and tooling costs can be amortized over long runs and that presses can be scheduled for maximum efficiency.

In contrast, Japanese practice is to locate stamping presses with the as-sembly plants, which requires dies to be changed often. This practice, in conjunc-tion with a Just-in-Time inventory philosophy, has forced the production and en-gineering people to develop the capability for short production runs, while con-serving capital. These intentional pressures on management have led to systemat-

ic progress in reducing obstacles to nimble plant operation, and one result has
been the dramatic drop in die change time. Other implications for product design,
efficiency, and plant scheduling also arise from the policy of locating stamping
and assembly plants in the same vicinity. More interesting, perhaps, is the fact
that differences in comparative industry structure arise in part from a Japanese
philosophy that treats characteristics of press operation as a challenge and an
opportunity for progress rather than as a given or a constraint.

Unionism at Tōyō Kōgyō

It is not possible to visit automotive plants in Japan and not come away
impressed with the teamwork and concentration evident on the shop floor. Our
visit at Tōyō Kōgyō included meetings with workers and officers of the Tōyō
Kōgyō union and gave us an opportunity to examine traditional explanations of
work force performance. Frank discussions about the real function of the union in
Japanese industry began to clarify the depth of the much-touted paternalistic
practices of Japanese management. What services does your union provide that
make it worth the dues you pay? If managers actually treat workers as fellow
members of the company, what need is there for a strong and expensive union?
The candid answers offered by workers and union members to these questions were
interesting and varied:

> "The union is essential to protect the workers from capricious deci-
> sions by management."
> "There are times when management tries to force higher output rates
> even when they haven't made their investment contribution."
> "They sometimes expect workers to do it all."
> "The union must constantly *remind* management that the worker de-
> serves his share of the economic gains that are reaped by the success-
> ful Japanese auto firms."

Despite these expressions of underlying suspicion, however, there was an
absence of the bitterness that often marks the adversarial relationships between
union and management in U. S. auto plants. One explanation for the absence of
bitterness is the narrow wage differential between managers and senior workers.
Another is the absence of the strong demarcation in status symbols that distinguish workmen from managers in U. S. plants. This was particularly noticeable in
regard to dress codes, access to plant facilities and some membership rules.
First-line supervisors, lower level managers, engineers, salespersons, office workers and most other staff personnel, for instance, are members of the union in
Japan. While U. S. managers might see the inclusion of such broadly defined
groups in the bargaining unit as a definite leftward tilt, Japanese executives understood it more as a moderating element for the union, than a concession to encourage the formulation of a powerful collective bargaining unit. Many of the

aspiring young managers we talked with look forward during their careers to a tour of duty as an officer in their company's union. The reasonableness of such an expectation is confirmed by the fact that one out of four chief executive officers in large Japanese firms have previously served as union officials.

Compared to the U. S. situation, the union in Japan is more like an arm of a company's personnel department than of the UAW. The union does get involved in grievances and does protect workers from capricious action, but a great deal of its resources are devoted to personnel functions like surveying salesworkers to discover sources of dissatisfaction or arranging for marriage ceremonies and helping to finance them. At the same time, the relationship between the union and the firm is quite a bit like the relationship between the marketing department and the production department or a well-managed corporation. There are differences of viewpoint, political infighting, and even strong words on occasion, but both groups share an understanding that the viability and prosperity of the firm are paramount.

The claim of U. S. union leaders that Japanese unions are soft on management finds some support if conditions in Japan are compared to the United States. But it is well to remember that the economic gains which the Japanese worker has realized through his collective bargaining process are not insubstantial. It is obvious, however, that the relationship between the Japanese union and the firm is much different than in the United States. In terms of implications for productivity and production effectiveness the Japanese worker could be expected to be more compliant than the U. S. worker with management objectives, given the structural situation in which he works. While unions provide some representation for their workers in traditional economic and work-rule matters, they fail to provide the same avenue for social change—for better or worse—as in the United States.

We departed Tōyō Kōgyō with new insights, with a feeling of warmth for our hosts, but with a sense that more questions had been raised than answered by our first set of plant visits. The initial sense of sameness in the technology had been matched by a sense of radicalness in the philosophy of workforce management. These feelings were to be reinforced by subsequent visits.

Mitsubishi, Honda and Toyota: Extensions of Initial Impressions

Our visit to Tōyō Kōgyō was followed by several days in the Nagoya area, where we visited Mitsubishi, Honda, and Toyota. Many impressions formed in Hiroshima were strengthened and reinforced in these other companies, but the opportunity to see the same operations in different environments highlighted important contrasts among the Japanese producers themselves. In Nagoya and in later visits to Nissan, we saw remarkable differences in process design and philosophy and equally large differences in atmosphere.

Mitsubishi was first on our Nagoya agenda. As we drove from Nagoya, the hustle and bustle of the modern urban center gave way to the quiet pastoral setting for Mitsubishi's Okazaki assembly and stamping plant, located about forty-five minutes from Nagoya. Nestled in among the rice fields tilled in the ancient manner, the Okazaki plant contained some of the most interesting technology we saw in Japan.

In the stamping plant, the ominous strokes of the giant high-speed sheet-metal presses dominated the initial stages of our tour. Our patient guide helped us to understand how the periodic activities of the stamping plant were coordinated with the continuous flow body-welding and assembly operations by a system of Just-in-Time inventory. The captivating feature of the tour, however, centered on a very sophisticated integration of computerized control and computer-activated multimodel welding presses in the body building section. The variety of models that were run down the common automated body assembly line was truly impressive. Only in Ford's Ohio truck plant (new in 1975) had we previously seen a level of sophistication in computer-integrated body automation in the United States that matched or bettered this process.

In the mixed-model assembly lines, cars that do not share a great deal of part commonality are assembled in a specified sequence on the same line. Such plants are common in Japan. Discussions in several companies suggested that the mixed-model line provided variety in the work, an important factor, we were told, in keeping workers interested in their work, and allowed the company to offer a richer product mix, at lower volumes, and without inefficient levels of investment. Yet even here we found exceptions. Honda, for example, operates some of its assembly plants with mixed models; others, however, are dedicated to a single model, particularly during short periods of time (e.g., a week or a month).

The mixed-model approach creates a broader range of tasks for the worker, but the extent of those tasks depends on process techniques and philosophy. To illustrate the very wide differences we found, consider the door-mounting operation. This is a critical task. It determines the fit of the door, its alignment with the body, how it sounds when closed, and so forth. Managers in the industry now recognize that the fit of the door is an important element in the buyer's assessment of the fit and finish of the car. At the Okazaki plant, the door-mounting operation was quite simple. As the body moved into position, a worker removed a door from a rack and bolted it onto the frame at the hinges. The worker then opened and shut the door to test its swing and then stood back and eyeballed the alignment. If it was not just right, the worker pulled out a rubber head mallet and whacked the door a few times in strategic locations until the door fit properly. All of this took about a minute.

The contrast with Nissan's Zama facility could not be sharper. Doors are mounted twice in the Zama process. Just after the body frame line, doors are bolted to the frames in a very quick operation. The purpose is not to mount the door, but to get the paint operation right; only one bolt is used at this stage. After painting, the doors are removed from the body and trimmed separately from the rest of the car. The real door-mounting operation takes place at the end of final assembly. As the almost complete car moves toward the end of the line, its doors (fully trimmed) are inserted into a sophisticated door-mounting device which positions the door while a worker bolts it on. There are no rubber mallets or sharp eyes in this approach; the machine fits the door.

The trade-offs implicit in these choices are instructive. Mitsubishi values the simplicity and low capital investment in their approach. Nissan wants the inside of the car assembled without the doors on and therefore has chosen to assemble components to the door separately. Once assembled, however, the door is more difficult to mount and align manually, and so a piece of equipment has been developed to do the job.

We found differences like this everywhere we went. They seem to arise from differences in philosophy, but also from a drive to find a competitive edge in the manufacturing process. Honda, for example, places emphasis on attaining high-quality production while maintaining rapid line speeds. The assembly plant we visited at Honda typically produces sixty-five cars per hour on a given assembly line. At Nissan, however, the philosophy is different. Nissan believes in slow line speeds (typically thirty cars per hour) and short assembly lines. Work tasks are longer and more varied than at Honda, and the process appears to be somewhat more capital intensive.

This brief discussion of the differences among the companies suggests some caution in generalizing about "the" Japanese auto industry. Each company has its own approach, its own atmosphere and culture. Yet it is also true that several aspects of the production process were common among the firms. Perhaps the most important was the management of inventory. Everywhere we went the iron-clad discipline of the Kanban/Just-in-Time inventory system governed the flow of inventory and product. While some of the notoriety the Kanban/Just-in-Time system has received can be chalked up to public relations, especially by Toyota, there are real and quite fundamental differences in the approach, differences which deserve to be highlighted.

A Behavioral System of Inventory

According to most conventions in the United States, the proper level of inventory is the one that balances the economic risk of disruption (e.g., set-up

costs, line stops) against the cost of carrying enough inventory to avoid the disruption. The choice of a particular level is simply a matter of applying the proper
calculus to the constraints and givens in a production process. As we came to
understand the Japanese view, however, inventory took on a new meaning. It is a
reservoir where problems may hide. When inventory floats are reduced to a low
level, problems with any given operation in the production process are likely to be
seen sooner. The weak link in a chain will not be apparent until the chain is drawn
taut.

Lowering inventory levels makes the sources of production problems apparent, be they long set-up times, erratic performance, poor equipment, or just plain
sloppy work. Problem visibility is increased and the consequences of failure become more severe. As inventory levels are lowered, workers and managers face
intensified pressure to work more closely as a team and to solve the problems that
impede more efficient flows. Thus inventory levels actually control the level of
stress on performance applied to the work force.

Based on our own observations in plant after plant, the level of stress that
the Japanese auto worker faces is actually quite high. In practice, of course, as
problems are worked out over time, inventory levels can be systematically
lowered to maintain a constantly high expectation for performance. And this
seems to be the case.

Stress, of course, need not always result in high-level performance. Yet we
found the two in combination in Japanese plants. In order to understand how the
Japanese producers achieve this result, an analogy may be helpful. Consider the
case of Mario Andretti's pit crew during the Indianapolis 500 (we owe this analogy
to Earl Sasser). Here we have a group of people working under conditions of
enormous stress, performing superbly. How do they do it? First, both the objective and the crew's role in the objective are clear-cut. They know that small differences in time spent in the pits can make the difference between winning and
losing. Second, the members of the crew are highly trained, not only in their individual functions but also in their work as a team. Hours are spent in working
together to develop better ways of handling their task. Third, the crew has good
support. They have equipment that functions well, and they have the benefit of a
system of operation developed over many years. Finally, there is a camaraderie
and esprit de corps that grow out of working together under pressure.

The analogy suggests that a high level of pressure for performance will only
lead to higher levels of performance in those cases where the people affected feel
that the stress is fair and acceptable in terms of their own values and where the
means of achievement is seen to rest in their hands.

The problem of winning a race on the speedway has advantages over making
cars. The stress on the crew derives from the situation itself and is not unfair;

everyone involved—drivers, mechanics, crew members—feels the same pressure. Values are not a problem, since there is a large element of self-selection, and only those who feel that auto racing is good and that winning is an appropriate goal get involved. And it is clear that the pit crew has the means to achieve its objective. Indeed, the driver relies on the crew for new ideas and methods, and equipment and support are provided as needed.

But even in a pit crew, good performance is not automatic. The process has to be managed. Equipment has to be developed or acquired. People have to be recruited, trained, and compensated. And the esprit de corps has to be nurtured. Similar tasks face the manager of an automobile production process who wants to get pit-crew-like performance out of his operation. However, the inherent structure of the situation (i.e., technology and work tasks) requires overcoming some major barriers. Perhaps the most important of these lies in the objectives of the operation and the worker's role in achieving those objectives. Winning the Indy 500 is one thing; increasing the rate of return on stockholders' equity quite another.

Since the plants we saw in Japan seemed to have a pit-crew quality, we were very interested in discussing the content of company training programs with the Japanese managers we visited. It did not take us long to learn that, along with training in substantive skills, considerable emphasis was also placed on instilling individual values that were coherent with the goals of the firm and an industrial society. Employees are exhorted to produce effectively for themselves and their family, their immediate coworkers, the broader corporate family, the community in which they live and their nation.

While the executives and workers we spoke with seemed every bit as interested in financial performance as their U. S. counterparts, the imagery of global combat, of a battle for leadership in world markets, subtly infused our conversations. Obviously, Japanese automobile workers do not weld the metal and bolt on the fenders with a patriotic (company and nation) song on their lips, a lump in their throat, and tears in their eyes. It is much more subtle. But there does seem to be a shared belief, instilled in training sessions and rituals and supported by company policy, that the quality of each day's work is not only essential to the survival of the company, but also an important factor in the nation's battle for position and standing in world affairs.

This important, if subtle, emphasis on beliefs and values is backed up by management policies and practices that place responsibility at low levels in the organization and that create the conditions for supportive small group activities. Quality circles have become something of a fad in the United States and Europe, where many firms have treated the concept as the means to achieve breakthroughs in quality and productivity. In contrast, while we found that the Japanese firms we visited treated quality circles as an important element in their overall approach to production, they tended to view formal quality circles as one of the last things to put in place after a lot of other things had been done. The importance of worker involvement and the role of small group activities are well-illustrated by our visit to Toyota's Takaoka assembly plant.

The White Eagles

Early one morning we attended a meeting of a seven-man quality circle from the trim line at the Takaoka assembly plant. The group had just come off the night shift. The White Eagles, as they named themselves, began their work in determined form, despite their obvious fatigue from the night's work. The group picked up in the middle of a project they had selected to work on many months before. This was their fourth or fifth meeting on the same project in roughly the same number of months.

The problem was to mount the correct door gasket on special cars. The problem job was done by one or two of the workers in this group. It was to put the gasket—the rubber seal into which the side door seats to make an air-tight closure—around the door. When the project was started, the group missed as many as seven per month. They simply failed either to select the right gasket or to note the ticket. Consequently they put the wrong gasket on the car. The group had already changed their job layout to reduce the chance of picking up the wrong gasket and had made other improvements based on their group deliberations at earlier meetings. As their control chart showed, the group's earlier work had borne fruit. The error rate had been forced down to one per month. The remaining error occurred on a cold weather metal, which required a special gasket.

The group worked to rid their jobs of this one error. They talked about how they could better notice the ticket (misreading the ticket seemed to be a major problem). A suggestion was made to relocate the job ticket from the end of the car to the side, where the gasket had to be mounted. They talked about going to the point in the line where fellow workers put the ticket on the car and asking the quality circle there about such relocation possibilities. This and other suggestions were discussed for about forty-five minutes and ultimately a new approach was agreed upon. At the end of the meeting we asked a few questions.

The most fascinating exchange concerned how they had selected their QC project. It seems that on their own initiative they had gone to the quality control group at the end of the line. From these people they had found the most frequent source of defect that originated from their area (i.e., the gasket problem). From this point they proceeded to track their performance on their own, to discuss the problem, and then to implement a solution. Of course management's permission to make changes had to be sought as required, but the entire process appeared to be self-starting and self-implementing.

Throughout our visits we found hundreds of quality circle groups doing what is essentially "methods engineering" on their own jobs and on their own time. Management provided the training and education to help them do it better, and managers evaluated the performance of the groups. Although part of the benefit of these small group activities was social and psychological in nature, the ideas and suggestions coming out of these efforts were an integral aspect of the improvement of productivity and quality in the plants we visited.

Technology and Automation: Where Are All the Robots?

Our foray into the world of the Japanese automobile plant began with the impression of technological sameness vis-a-vis the United States and, at the same time, a sense of radical difference in the management of people and materials. These initial impressions were confirmed in each of the companies we visited. Having been conditioned by magazine articles and newspaper stories about advanced technology, we found ourselves wondering where all the robots were. To be sure, the Japanese make use of more robots in spot welding than is the case in the United States, but the differences were not breathtaking. Indeed, technology does not appear to be as important a factor in explaining the Japanese edge in quality and productivity as is widely assumed. Our impressions about technology are well illustrated by our visits to Toyota's Kamigo engine plant and Nissan's Zama assembly plant.

The Kamigo four-cylinder engine plant was built and tooled circa 1965. It was of particular interest since we had only recently visited the most modern engine plant in Detroit, which had sophisticated 1980 tooling and which also produced a similar engine. In aggregate totals, however, the Detroit plant is budgeted at about twice as many labor hours per engine as the Kamigo plant. Despite the Detroit plant's elegant systems for laser inspections of machined parts, complex feedback and control for machine tools, and the very latest and best processing machines that money could buy, the fact remains that the fifteen-year-old Japanese plant offers twice the labor productivity. With freedom to inspect operations in both plants we convinced ourselves that both manufactured roughly the same number of the engines' subordinate parts and that the enormous gap in productivity was not due to a trick, like the use of extensive vendor labor in the plant.

Our Kamigo visit underscored the point that advanced technology does not necessarily imply superior performance. The Japanese plant was fifteen years older than its U. S. counterpart. More myths were shattered in our visit to Zama. Few plants in the world have attained the notoriety of Nissan's Zama facility. Pictures of a car body surrounded by an army of robots, together with claims that most of the work in the plant is done by robots, have created the image of a space-age plant run by machines. (An April 23, 1980, story in the *Milwaukee Journal* was entitled: "Robots Do the Work on Datsuns.") The reality, however, is quite different. Most of the robots at Zama are used in the body shop, where sheet-metal parts are welded to form the body. The welding operations are automated to a significant extent, but the rest of the plant did not contain advanced technology. In fact, our calculations suggest that the Zama facility may be somewhat less productive than some of the other assembly plants we visited.

While the level of automation in the body shop was significant, the shop was not operated as we expected it to be. At Zama, the painting operation is scheduled separately from final assembly and therefore uses a large (100 cars) buffer inventory before and after paint. When this queue fills, the body line, with all of its tooling and robotics, shuts down because the line is not synchronized with the lines it is feeding. During these periodic shutdowns, workers perform minor cleaning and maintenance on the welding equipment. Our discussions with Nissan managers suggest that they are more concerned about the quality of the painting and welding than about efficient use of capital.

Whatever the specific reason behind the methods of operations, it is clear that advanced robotics is but a small part of the explanation for the performance of the Zama facility. We do not mean to imply that good equipment skillfully used and maintained is not important at Zama or at other facilities. In fact, in the Kamigo plant, the high level of material handling between transfer lines and at other stations is done by machine, primarily very simple devices using principles such as gravity feed. Our conclusion after seeing a variety of processes was that it is not so much differences in the level of technological sophistication that accounts for superior performance; it is the way that the technology is managed.

The Suppliers

Any discussion of the Japanese auto industry and its approach to production would be incomplete without some analysis of the suppliers. It only takes ten minutes inside an assembly plant in Japan to realize that relationships with suppliers are very different. The visitor accustomed to the loading docks, the large storage areas, and the large incoming inspection area typical of U. S. plants is likely to be taken aback by the stocking of Japanese assembly lines. Trucks from suppliers back up through large bay doors right to the assembly line; supplier personnel unload a few hours worth of parts, clean up the area, and depart. There is no incoming inspection, no staging area, no fork lift trucks, no expediting of material, just a seemingly continuous flow of material. Suppliers have to have significant production capabilities, or the system will not work.

We visited several suppliers during our trip and came away with several impressions. Clearly, many of the firms we saw (e.g., Nippondensō) have become very large and capable firms in their own right. We found no evidence of what some Kanban critics claim—that the OEMs had shifted inventories back to suppliers; of course, we may not have been able to go far enough back in the chain. However, we did find evidence of substantial quality control efforts at the supplier level. It was also clear that the OEMs devote significant resources (management and technical) to sustaining and improving supplier capability. The relationships are long-term and involve an exchange of people, know-how, and capital.

The visits to suppliers placed the pros and cons of such stable long-term supplier relationships into sharp perspective. A solid technological base, growing competence in quality control and equipment modernization offer testimony to the benefits of stable and supportive procurement and supply relationships. Such relationships very obviously gave the suppliers the confidence, information, stability of objective, and, of course, the capital to modernize their operations. At the same time, of course, suppliers may fall victim to the forces of technological change in the components they produced. The world's most advanced mechanical gauge (e.g., speedometers, fuel gauges) assembly line, for example, may be rendered obsolete in a world of electronic monitoring devices. What does the supportive OEM do with the supplier who has failed to keep abreast of major developments in new technology? The response of the U. S. auto firm in many instances might be to seek out a new supplier. We could not tell how long a Japanese OEM would support a technologically lagging supplier.

Policies that doggedly foster only supportive long-term relationships raised a question about the vulnerability of the Japanese OEM-supplier "family" to competitively imposed technological change. The question of competitive performance under conditions of technological uncertainty remains unanswered because the Japanese economy has yet to be extensively tested in this respect.

We did find, however, that in the course of normal technological progress, where product change is not radical but evolutionary, the Japanese suppliers and OEMs appear to have some important advantages. Chief among these is their approach to capital equipment. Without exception, every firm we visited had a highly developed capability to produce some of its own capital equipment—in particular, machine tools. In the typical case, the suppliers we visited had developed the core manufacturing technology on which their competitive position rested. For example, Nihon Radiator, a company that produced radiators for Nissan, developed a unique machine for manufacturing radiator fins as well as other critical machinery for its manufacturing process. The same was true of each producer we visited. (We had previously noted this same tendency among West German auto suppliers.) Part of the genius behind excellence in product development for efficient production is an intimate understanding of the technological possibilities of production. We have found that firms in the U. S. auto industry differ from both Japanese and West German firms in this regard. In our opinion, such differences help account for the excellent flexibility of German and Japanese firms in accommodating product change with capital efficiency.

The development of an in-house equipment manufacturing capability shortens lead times and accommodates product diversity. Production of capital equipment provides skill and insight both in designing products that can be flexibly tooled and, more directly, in designing the flexible tooling itself. In addition, it helps promote a closer relationship between product and manufacturing design groups so that "manufacturability" is considered from the inception of the design process. This, of course, is also aided by cross-functional career paths and by other policies that enhance interfunctional cooperation. Here, as in other aspects of production, the management of people plays a fundamental role.

II. Interpretations

What does this account of Japanese policies and practices add up to? Do the techniques of inventory management, work force management, task design, and so forth amount to nothing more than a collection of isolated, albeit effective, practices? Or are there overarching principles that inform them all? If so, how applicable might they be to other economies and industrial cultures? To consider these questions it is instructive to examine the practices we have seen in the context of the competitive strengths of Japanese industry.

In high-volume, capital-intensive industries like automobiles or appliances, almost any prioritized list of Japan's competitive strengths would certainly include the following:

1. Very high labor productivity (one-half to two-thirds U. S. labor content);
2. High product quality;
3. Short procreation times in new product development; and
4. A capacity to accommodate great product diversity in production.

There is much less agreement about the sources of these strengths than there is about the strengths themselves. Single factor explanations abound. Japanese industry has the most up-to-date plant and equipment! Its capital stock is newer! Japanese workers are more disciplined! Japanese management takes a longer-range point of view! Japanese culture supports respect for authority! The Japanese manager pays great attention to detail! The interested observer who seeks some understanding is literally deluged with buzzwords and a variety of "secrets to Japan's success."

Of course many of these single factor explanations contain elements of truth, but they are far from satisfying as an explanation of Japanese competitive strengths. In fact, our trip observations show that some of them are just plain misleading. With regard to the "modern plant and equipment" argument, for example, we have even reported contradictory evidence. In Toyota's Kamigo engine plant, labor productivity is much higher than it is in U. S. plants with ultramodern equipment producing comparable products. Here an unremodeled technology that is one and one-half decades old outperforms the latest U. S. technology. Similarly, the supposedly culturally compliant Japanese worker sees the same need for union protection against his "paternalistic" firm as does the U. S. worker. Further, we find that in Japanese industries where labor markets and attractive incentives for job switching do exist (e.g., electronics and computer programming), Japanese workers voluntarily give up lifetime employment and "job hop," just like their U. S. counterparts. Nor is there always labor peace: witness the acrimonious Japanese strikes at the end of World War II.

Sources of Quality and Productivity Advantages

After intensive study of the auto industry in Japan, after extensive discussions with a variety of people in the U. S. industry, and after comparative analysis of practices and methods in the major producing countries around the world, it is our judgment that the Japanese edge in quality and productivity cannot be attributed to any single factor. Rather, a number of diverse aspects appear to be significant. If asked to name the principal immediate sources of the production/quality gap, our short list would look like this:

1. lines operate a higher percentage of the time (less down time due to maintenance)
2. greater use of material handling equipment
3. fewer defective parts
4. lower absenteeism
5. job design and job structure (broadly trained workers perform more effectively)
6. more work per year per worker (more time spent on the job, and a faster work pace)

Although the factors listed are varied, it would be a mistake to assume that they are independent or unrelated. Indeed, it is important to look for that which links apparently diverse sources of advantage to one another. For example, while the policy of Just-in-Time production and the reduction of work-in-progress inventories are not listed as direct sources of Japan's productivity advantage, it is our view that they are critical enabling factors. These policies provide stimulus for identifying production problems early; they help to make worker performance visible in a social sense; and they contribute to a more cohesive and team-oriented work force orientation. Cohesiveness among coworkers is further supported by management-structured small group activities, by delegation of authority to low levels in the organization (sometimes called quality circles), and by personnel practices like lifetime employment, seniority-oriented promotion, and so forth. Of course, this cohesiveness affects productivity and quality indirectly through its implications for reduced absenteeism and greater interest in the job. What lies at the heart of Japan's observed excellence in manufacturing is the coherence and consistency in all the aspects of its production system.

It is our view that the cause of the differences between U. S. and Japanese practices, the theme which links all of them, is the integration of the individual worker (blue or white collar) into the production process. In the context of a production philosophy in which the elimination of waste and the pursuit of excellence is paramount, the Japanese producers have turned work force management into a major competitive weapon.

Work Force Management as a Strategic Competitive Factor

In recent years the U. S. philosophy in the design and the management of production processes has been to treat all the factors of production, including inputs of labor, capital, raw materials, and components, as a system of input commodities that are to be purchased and sold as required to optimize the performance of the process. The U. S. philosophy represents a transaction approach both to the design of the production process and to its management. In contrast, the Japanese philosophy treats the work force and its organization as a resource with dynamic competitive capabilities that may be developed, nurtured, and shaped into a competitive weapon.

Table 1 summarizes the seven practices or "Pillars of Japanese Work Force Management" typically followed by the Japanese automobile producers we visited to utilize their work force more completely as a competitive weapon. As in the case of process design, firms differ in their approach to managing people, and the practices vary from company to company. Yet the basic approach and philosophy are quite similar.

Each difference between Japanese and U. S. practice reflects a behavioral viewpoint about that policy's effect on work force performance. The scope of these differences is broad and involves approaches to vendor relations, work-in-process inventory, equipment maintenance, facility layout, quality circle organization and so forth. We do not mean to suggest that Japanese policies are designed to promote giddy on-the-job happiness among workers. To the contrary, we find that the way the Japanese have integrated their work force into the production process burdens the worker with much of the same competitive stress manage-

Table 1
SEVEN PILLARS OF
JAPANESE WORK FORCE MANAGEMENT

1. Worker-oriented conditions of employment supported by "Corporate Family" concept, through:

> The security of lifetime employment
> Company-sponsored housing, stores, recreational facilities, etc.
> Equitable policies in promotion that emphasize seniority over fast tracks

2. Reduced symbols of status differences among managers and workers as a result of:

> Pay grades largely based on seniority
> Equal access to corporate facilities and services

3. Job enrichment by the vertical enlargement of work assignment, through:

> Inclusion of equipment maintenance functions in the operators' tasks
> Incorporating methods and task improvement responsibility in job assignment (sometimes through quality circle activities)
> Extensive training to provide knowledge and skills for the above

4. Workers' job performance on routine tasks is made highly visible through:

> Physical design of the work place and its environment
> Minimized work-in-progress inventories

5. Harmonized values of worker's unions vis-a-vis those of management by:

> A broadly defined collective bargaining unit including engineers' staffs, etc.
> Interchangeable roles among union leadership and management

6. Managed small group activities that reinforce positive attitudes toward the job through:

> Quality circle or equivalent activities
> Work group training and recreational activities

7. Value training vis-a-vis the employees' responsibility to fellow workers, the customer, the corporate family, the community and society

ment faces. In return, the Japanese worker sees himself or herself as a more vital, more effective member of the organization.

A management system that challenges workers to perform and provides the necessary support while raising the social consequences of failure seems to be socially rewarding for the workers as well as competitively successful for the firm. The Japanese system may tap 15 to 20 percent of the typical worker's potential as a member of the organization; the U. S. approach gains at best 5 to 10 percent of that potential. The success of Japanese producers of automobiles and other products and the experience of Japanese-managed plants in this country suggest that the philosophy and practices depicted in Table 1 constitute a new "one-best-way" in work force management.

The importance of the Japanese work force management system to the competitive strengths of their industry was brought into focus again and again throughout the trip. In instance after instance, we talked with senior executive about barriers to foreign competitive challenges. For example, we asked if industry in Korea or Taiwan might some day mount a challenge from their lower-cost industrial base much as the Japanese firms had challenged U. S. markets. The answer was almost always the same: "We believe that the special skills of Japanese workers and the particular ability they have to handle complex technological productivity will provide the needed competitive barriers to entry." One senior Japanese manager made the point in a very personal way. "As an individual you may be smarter than I am; but once I begin to work within my organization with my fellow workers, I am unbeatable." We concur that the Japanese approach to work force organization is indeed effective.

Yet it is important to realize that the Japanese auto producers have not discovered the manufacturer's Nirvana. The specific practices and policies through which these seven basic principles have been implemented assume social, economic, and technological stability. The future, however, may well be much less stable in these respects than the past has been. The work force in Japan is aging substantially, and expectations are rising as the levels of education and living standards rise. At the same time, it is unlikely that the auto producers can sustain the kind of growth they have experienced in recent years. The future may include growing social demands coupled with fluctuations in demand that will place strains on current practices. The relative prices of oil and gas may also rise, creating incentives for substantial changes in product technology. The technological environment may grow increasingly fluid and uncertain, creating the need for marked changes in processes and methods. The Japanese executives we spoke with are aware of these problems and view them—and the competitive actions which grow out of them—as a major challenge for the future.

III. Conclusions

At the beginning of this report, we quoted Taiichi Ohno, the architect of Toyota's production system. He drew an analogy between Toyota's approach to production and the early policies that Henry Ford followed in creating the U. S. auto industry at the turn of the century. The analogy is perceptive; it shows an understanding of the relationship among inventory, precision, and productivity not shared by most U. S. managers. The very idea sounds a bit farfetched. Ohno asks us to believe that the relatively exotic, arcane practices followed by most Japanese auto producers are not mysterious at all, but rather precisely what a youthful Henry Ford would have done. It is our judgment that Mr. Ohno is substantially correct. The development of the Model T and the "Ford Shops and Methods" reveals a fascinating pattern of similarities and contrasts with the Japanese producers of the modern era. Like the Japanese today, the Ford factories of the pre-World War I era attracted widespread attention and sparked a variety of visits and studies. On a technical level, Ford managers and engineers integrated and synchronized a collection of disparate operations and organized them in sequence. The objective was progressive or continuous production. H. L. Arnold, an industrial journalist of that era, described progressive production in terms reminiscent of descriptions we heard in Japan:

> the scheme of placing both machine and hand work in straight line sequence of operations, so that the component in progress will travel the shortest road from start to finish, with no avoidable handling whatsoever.

Although the popular conception of Ford's breakthrough has emphasized the moving assembly line, in fact this was only one part of a synthesis of new production concepts. It is that synthesis which mirrors the Japanese approach. Indeed, Ford's vigorous emphasis on the design and fabrication of advanced machine tools, his relentless drive to rationalize production and reduce in-process inventories, his emphasis on productivity gains through continuous process flows, his reliance on simple material handling equipment, and his focus on precision machining in a simple design all parallel current Japanese practices.

Behind the development of an integrated, specialized, standardized production process lay a basic philosophy of the "factory as laboratory." It is clear from the historical record that there was no grand design, no once-and-for-all blueprint that Ford put into effect. There was, however, a commitment to learn from experience and to change and develop the process to make it more efficient. Ford's frequent comment that his research laboratory was his factory reflected a commitment to evolutionary progress and operational continuity. His relentless process rationalization drove total inventories at Ford (including raw material and distribution inventories from 204 days of inventory in 1903 to 17 days in the heyday of Model T production in 1922. This was achieved despite extensive backward integration into the production of iron, steel, rubber, wood, and fabric.

Even the very low inventories found in well-managed Japanese automobile plants pale in comparison to the rationalization achieved at the Rouge River complex. Documentary evidence from the 1920s shows that a load of iron ore delivered to the Rouge River docks was typically processed through the blast furnace, taken through casting, rough and finish machining, and assembly in about forty-eight hours. Here was integrated production! Two days from iron ore to finished product! Japanese practice has not extended process rationalization too far beyond the state of the art that was established in Ford's Rouge River facility during the 1920s. Indeed, recent Japanese productivity gains have paralleled those achieved at Ford during approximately the same number of years.

The rationalization of production at Ford was accompanied by—indeed it necessitated—innovative approaches to work force management. It is here, in the management of people and their integration into the production process, that we find fascinating parallels but ultimately sharp contrasts to the Japanese. As in the modern Japanese auto plant, process rationalization at Ford created tremendous pressure on the shop floor. In a tightly integrated system there is the constant, consistent pressure for production. But at Ford in the early days, even though the problem wasn't fully identified, there was support for that pressure in a form that had interesting similarities to the Japanese system. In her psychoanalytic study of Henry Ford's leadership style, Dr. Anne Jardin writes of the early organization environment as follows:

> A man could make his own job, assume responsiblity where he felt fit. The job and how well it was done formed the basis of the relationship between Ford and his executives, none of whom was boss in any formal sense.
> To help suppliers cut costs, Ford sent engineers into their plants to improve manufacturing methods, (and) paid in advance for their products to give them capital for high-volume machine tools.
> In respect to the environment on the shop floor, even the relentless Ford critic, Keith Sward, acknowledges the camaderie that existed in the early years.[1]

By 1913, managers at Ford came to recognize that the "human element" in production needed substantial attention. John R. Lee, Ford's first labor manager, commented:

1. Anne Jardin, *The first Henry Ford: A study in personality and business leadership* (Cambridge, Mass.: The MIT Press, 1970), p. 204 and 91. See also Keith Sward, *The legend of Henry Ford* (New York: Reinhard & Co., 1948), p. 15-40.

we began to realize something of the relative value of men, mechanism and material, so to speak, and we confess that up to this time we believed that mechanism and material were of larger importance and that somehow or other the human element of our men was taken care of automatically and needed little or no consideration.

A variety of problems surfaced in the 1912-1913 period which proved that the Ford people did not learn this well enough or soon enough. High rates of turnover (370 percent per year), absenteeism, and output restriction all caused performance to be much less than expected. Coupled with the influx of immigrant workers, the problems inherent in the rationalized production process prompted a variety of experiments and changes in work force management.

The most famous innovation was the Five Dollar Day, which amounted to a form of profit sharing. Workers received their previous wage as base pay, and were allowed to "participate in the profits" up to five dollars per day if they met certain standards of sobriety, thriftiness, and hard work. But other policies reinforced and supplemented the Five Dollar Day in its attempt to create an incentive for behavior conducive to high-level performance. The Sociological Department was developed to investigate and shape the attitudes and habits of Ford employees and to instill a set of values compatible with industrial production. Adherence to the Ford Standards (e.g., living conditions, habits of thrift and sobriety) was a prerequisite for sharing in the profits; in addition, Ford promised that no one would be fired except for unfaithfulness or inefficiency. The company created a committee to review discharge cases, operated an English school, conducted a variety of welfare activities (e.g., gymnasium for workers, assistance to workers' families in distress), and generally sought to create a work force with the right attitudes, motivated to produce, and free of worries about home and family.

The innovations in process design at Ford changed the role of people in production, and created pressure for innovation in organizational conditions to support the high-level performance that came to be demanded of the workers. The policies developed at Ford were innovative and effective, at least as far as productivity was concerned. Turnover dropped rapidly in the wake of the Five Dollar Day, and labor hours per vehicle in assembly fell as well. While not all of the productivity growth can be chalked up to work force innovations, they were an important aspect.

The demands brought on by pressure for more production and lower costs were relentless, however. Twenty years of high-volume production, market booms and busts, and national criticism made their mark on Ford. The organizational conditions that were needed to support the enormous social stress generated by the giant economic system could not be maintained.

After World War I, paternalism at Ford gave way to anti-unionism, authoritarian shop control, and the infamous Service Department. The innovations in work force management at Ford between 1914 and 1918 could not be sustained as the basic approach to integrating people into the production process. Commitment to employee welfare, employment stability, profit sharing, and value training was supplanted by heavy-handed supervision and by the kind of adversarial relationship eventually codified in the union-organizing drives and contracts of the 1930s and 1940s. Productivity improvement and competitive effectiveness faltered.

We accept Mr. Ohno's word that he learned from the experiences of the first Henry Ford. For today's Japanese manager, however, we believe the relevant question is how much of the later lessons taught by Henry Ford's experience with difficulties in sustaining productivity improvement will prove to be applicable. Can the social conditions needed to sustain recent high rates of productivity improvement be maintained under the conditions of uncertainty which the future seems to portend?

For the U.S. manager, the relevant questions are different. How can we learn from the Japanese in a way consistent with our heritage? Some very real questions are raised about the piecemeal application of Japanese management concepts. The failure of these early practices to take hold at Ford illustrates the need for caution in blindly applying something like the "seven pillars" in the U.S. context. We do not mean that important lessons should not be learned from the Japanese, or for that matter, from the Ford experience. It is only that barriers exist and that specific policies for implementing the principles will have to be developed carefully. The challenge for U.S. management is not to imitate Japanese practices, but to understand their underpinnings and to learn from this experience.

PARTICIPATIVE WORK PRACTICES
IN THE JAPANESE AUTO INDUSTRY:
SOME NEGLECTED CONSIDERATIONS

Yoshitaka Fujita

It is my great honor and pleasure to be invited here to talk with you on Quality Control, or QC, circle activities and other forms of participatory work practices in the Japanese auto industry. It is generally believed that these practices have had a revolutionary impact on the attitudes of Japanese auto workers toward job performance, and that they have contributed much to increased productivity and the improved quality of Japanese cars.

However, it is not so widely known that Japanese auto management encountered many problems while introducing and operating QC circles. Before QC circles were introduced in the early 1960s, Japanese auto workers were accustomed to a passive "Do as you are told" style of work operation. This was associated with our permanent employment and seniority wage practices. In many respects these practices have a positive effect. They do not, however, contain direct incentives for improved job performance. It is appropriate to say, then, that Japanese auto management, with constant effort, succeeded in adopting QC circles *in spite of* traditional industrial relationships, or Japanese culture.

Today, in the 1980s, Japanese auto management is facing a new set of problems for effective operation of QC circles. Difficulties are arising from the introduction of industrial robots, from the aging of the labor force, young workers' leisure-oriented values, and other environmental and cultural changes. As in the case of the 1960s, we can say that Japanese auto management is making a continuous effort to succeed in motivating workers *in spite of* these problems.

Finally, it is important to point out that the QC circle, and almost all other participative work practices now widely utilized in the Japanese auto industry, was originally invented and practically applied in the United States. Japan bor-

Yoshitaka Fujita is a Professor in the Faculty of Economics, Asia University, Tokyo, Japan.

rowed them, and developed them in Japanese ways. For example, Mr. Eiji Toyoda, President of Toyota Motor Company, and the first Japanese auto industrialist after World War II permitted to visit the United States to study engineering, told me that in the late 1940s he brought back to Toyota the Ford Motor Company's "suggestion system." That was the beginning of the suggestion system in Japan. His statement, "If America could, why not Japan?" was the idea and the impetus for Japanese management to import participative work practices from the United States.

Today, as in the past, we pay respect to positive American efforts to deal with auto trade problems by increasing productivity and improving the quality of American automobiles.

Now I would like to turn to some neglected considerations in an overall view of QC circle activity in Japan.

1. First: QC circle activity is only one form of a wide variety of participative practices in the Japanese auto industry.

Contrary to what some Americans seem to believe, QC circle activity does not exist in a vacuum. Nor is it necessarily central to participative activities in the auto industry. QC circle activity is woven into a wide network of practices such as job enlargement, job enrichment, multiskill career development and training, job rotation, suggestion system, profit sharing, informal human relations, group activities through sports, recreational and cultural clubs, worker welfare programs, community activities, and so on. All of these are commonly observed at Toyota, Nissan, Tōyō Kōgyō, Mitsubishi, Honda, and other auto companies in Japan.

For example, Total Quality Control (TQC) circle activity was introduced at Toyota in 1966. Today, almost all Toyota personnel, from top management through the rank and file, belong to one of many TQC circles. It is company policy to make each worker a versatile, multiskilled employee. Employees are rotated among several different jobs. Generally, assemblers change jobs once every one or two months, although rotation timing is not entirely rigid. Job training is actually on-the-job training and offered on a man-to-man basis.

Technical training and education are also provided through off-the-job training and education in basic knowledge. Techniques of scientific or statistical quality control are taught to all workers off-the-job during a period of about ten days a year. Many rank and file assembly workers are allowed to repair their own machines and equipment once they are designated by the engineering department. This is regarded as a great honor and serves as incentive for workers in ascending their career ladders.

The goal of job rotation and training is captured in the slogan "Whoever can do whatever jobs, wherever and whenever." In general, there are no job jurisdiction problems in Japanese industry. At work sites about ten workers, performing similar jobs as a unit team, are organized into one TQC circle. Each circle selects a leader, and leadership rotates in order to permit every worker the experience of the leadership role, and an understanding of the importance of the role of the follower.

The team discusses certain problems, determines a project, and sets up monthly, quarterly, or annual goals to achieve. This is usually done with the assistance of their foreman and the engineering staff. Then, the team's autonomous activity begins, as well as the search to identify specific problems and to study measures for solving them. When solutions are achieved, the team is encouraged to put them into practice. At this stage the foreman and engineering staff play a vital role. Informally, the foreman and the engineering department keep close contact with the QC circle. They advise the team on the proper direction for carrying out the solution in practice. This involves constant consultation with the engineering department.

After the solution has been successfully accomplished, the team presents its findings to the company's suggestion office for registration. In 1981, Toyota received 1,412,500 suggestions from 45,240 employees. This averaged more than 31 suggestions per worker. More than 95 percent were group suggestions; 94 percent were adopted. According to the financial statement to the stockholders of Toyota, about one-third of the increase in operating profit in 1981 was a result of these suggestions. Nissan received 1,267,222 suggestions from 53,941 employees, or 23 suggestions per employee, with an adoption rate of 90 percent. Nissan paid prize money of five million dollars in the same year. Nissan estimates these suggestions contributed to increased profit by thirty million dollars in 1980. Tōyō Kōgyō operates its Master Quality Circle activity and received 1,350,574 suggestions from 27,900 employees, or 48 suggestions per worker per year, in 1981. Honda operates its New Honda Circles and received 160,400 suggestions from 22,908 employees, or 7 suggestions per employee, in 1980.

Workers at Toyota perform their jobs while thinking of ways to upgrade the quality of those jobs. Product quality and material and energy conservation are currently emphasized in TQC circles. At Toyota, workers are called "Small Sakichi's," from the name of Toyota's founder, Sakichi Toyota, known as the king of invention in Japan—somewhat like your Thomas Edison. TQC circles are actually "small invention" groups. Participation in QC circles makes work enjoyable and satisfying. Quality is given priority on the Toyota assembly line. Each assembler is authorized to stop the line any time he recognizes it as necessary to maintain quality. He can and does push the "stop button" placed at each assembler's work station.

There is also a movement called "Help and Be Helped" among Toyota workers. There is no presetting of a rigid, standard work volume or job assignment to help individuals at Toyota factories. Those who complete a task more quickly help to complete the tasks of their coworkers, even when those tasks are different from the work they have been doing. In a spontaneous fashion the more able person covers the less able, and they all perform their jobs as a team. There is virtually no wall between jobs or workers. At the exit of each Toyota assembly plant there is a notice which reads, "Today you have produced a total of (X) number of cars. Thank you for your best cooperation."

Toyota workers also participate in a profit-sharing plan. There is a monthly bonus paid in the form of a group incentive bonus plan. In addition, there are the summer and winter bonuses, amounting in total to about six months' regular wages. These are also based on productivity performance.

As a support to these work practices at Toyota, there is also a network of informal activies in sports, recreational, and cultural clubs. Every worker belongs to at least one club of this kind, and most belong to several. Leaders of these clubs, most of whom are foremen and senior workers, together with new employees (in total about 500 employees) spend four days and five nights during summer vacation on a sea-study trip called "Toyota College on Cruise," which the company has sponsored for many years. The president and almost all top management people participate to exchange views with the workers directly. We can conclude that, first and foremost, QC circle and other forms of the participatory work practices in Japan are *people building.* In 1981, Toyota also contributed about twenty million dollars to establish the "Toyota Workers' Family Welfare Fund." The company did this jointly with the Toyota union.

There is also a vast network of QC circle activies for sharing information and gaining recognition. These activities occur not only at the plant level, but also at the corporate level, the regional level, and the national level. On an annual basis the best QC circle is selected at the plant level. It then represents the plant at the corporate-level circle meeting where the president of the firm attends and awards the prize to the best circle. This circle then represents the company at the regional and national QC circle conventions. Such representation is a great honor for the circle members involved. In addition the Deming prize is awarded annually to the company with the best quality performance. This is also a great honor for the company.

2. Second: There is a broad range of indirect participation in management through the union in the form of union-management joint consultation councils.

At the company, plant, and department levels, participative work practices are supported by a broad range of organizational activity which gives workers' indirect participation in management. This is achieved through the union-management joint consultation council. At Toyota, for example, top management and top union officials, including the presidents of both groups, meet regularly once every three months and at other times when necessary. In the central union-management joint consultation council, they meet to promote understanding, and to exchange views and information. They also discuss and consult in advance on almost every matter directly or indirectly concerned with workers. These include: long-range management plans, introduction of new technology, investment, production, overseas investment and operation, financial situations, market conditions, employment, personnel and welfare problems, pollution, public relations, and so on.

Even though the council is only for consultation, the fact is that top management seldom makes a decision to implement plans without the prior consent of the union. Contents of these council discussions are communicated to the rank-and-file union members. There are also several technical subcommittees established under the council. At the plant level, plant union-management joint consultation council meetings are held regularly once a month. Production schedules, manning, and working hours are main topics of discussion at these sessions.

At the department level, department union-management joint council meetings are held as needed. Production schedules, manning, working hours, productivity, quality, training, safety and hygiene, and recreational activities are major topics. Informal meetings among top management executives and rank-and-file workers, foremen, middle management personnel, engineers, and so on are often held during lunch or after work. It is common for Toyota executives to join groups of workers, eating dinner together at the company restaurant or dormitory. Such occasions provide an opportunity for explaining the company's long-range plans, budget, new technology, and market prospects directly to rank-and-file workers. At the same time, these executives listen to workers' opinions, suggestions, or complaints about various workplace problems.

Along with Toyota, Nissan and other auto companies follow a similar pattern of union-management joint consultation councils. However, such consultation councils do not necessarily guarantee industrial peace. Sometimes unions take tough stands and use council discussions to demand major improvements in safety and hygiene, or shorter work hours.

At the regional, industrial, and national level there are tripartite union-management Joint Consultation Councils.

3. Third: Participative work practices play a major role in Japanese auto parts
   supplier firms.

The quality of parts is a vital determinant in the quality of finished cars.
Japanese auto assembly makers maintain, on the one hand, very high quality standards for their parts suppliers, and provide, on the other hand, full technical and
managerial assistance to those suppliers. Auto manufacturers do not usually perform a detailed incoming inspection on the parts supplied. However, they do visit
the suppliers' factories, observe the work process and quality, and give advice. In
a sense, the parts are inspected at their origin. For example, Nissan promotes a
"3P" program—participation, productivity, and progress—among its parts suppliers. All QC circle movements adopted by Nissan parts suppliers are encouraged
and supported by Nissan. Nissan organized the Nissan Group QC, which is participated in by the top management, engineers, and QC circle leaders of sixty-three
suppliers. Nissan holds seminars regularly for the Nissan Group as a whole.
Nissan says the level of quality from their suppliers is currently better than their
own assembly operations.

In 1966, Toyota introduced the "All-Toyota Perfect Quality Program." This
program requires all Toyota-group parts suppliers to participate in the company's
quality control and reliability education courses. These are held annually for ten-
day periods, including engineers, managers, foremen, and QC circle leaders, re-
spectively. Each course has 100 participants. About 60 percent are from parts
supplier firms. QC circles have now spread to all Toyota-group parts makers as a
result of participation in these courses.

Toyota organizes and maintains an All-Toyota QC circle office involving
the company's fourteen major suppliers. At the "All-Toyota Annual QC Circle
Convention," the best circles representing Toyota and the suppliers report on the
results of circle activity. The convention is attended by presidents and other top
management, middle managers, engineers, and Circle leaders from each company. Indeed, the attention given to such activity by top management is a distinctive feature of the Japanese approach.

Toyota also presents its "Toyota Annual Deming Prize" to the best supplier
after an appraisal of QC circle activities among the supplier group. In the course
of checking and appraising, Toyota offers advice, consultation, and assistance for
improving quality in parts and management.

In summary, Toyota promotes quality control on an all-Toyota group-wide
basis, with activities ranging from education and training to appraisal of QC circle
results.

4. Fourth: It is clear that participative work practices have merit and produce results.

From the Japanese experience we can demonstrate that QC circle activity has been effective in a number of areas—in increasing productivity, upgrading product quality, conserving materials and energy, reducing cost, and motivating workers. On this last point, QC circle activity has enabled workers to become trained, educated, and multiskilled. The added benefit here has been reduced alienation and increased satisfaction with jobs and the workplace. It is not an exaggeration to say that the Japanese auto industry and, indeed, the Japanese economy would not be what they are today if there had been no QC circles or other participative activities. Today, the managers and workers of most companies including smaller ones believe that the introduction of QC circles will lead them to prosperity and that unless they do introduce QC circles, they face bankruptcy and unemployment.

5. Fifth: The strategic efforts of management and the cooperation of unions have led Japanese QC circle activity to success.

As we noted at the beginning, it is neither Japanese culture nor the Japanese national character that have produced QC circle success. Rather, it has been the strategic and long term efforts of Japanese management and the cooperation of workers and unions that have led to QC success. The scientific techniques and innovative spirit of the Foreman Quality Control, as well as Statistical Quality Control, have significantly changed Japanese workers. It was formerly said that Japanese workers "move well but don't work." Today they not only work well, but creatively.

There are several general factors which led Japanese management to introduce QC circles. Among them should be mentioned the democratization of Japanese education under the American occupation. This opened the way for ordinary people to obtain secondary and higher education. Group-study programs were also introduced in Japanese grade schools after the war. A second factor contributing to QC circle adoption was a traditional absence of job-jurisdictional practices in Japan. And third, both management and workers in the auto and other industries in Japan saw increased productivity and improved quality as the only way to survive the cut-throat domestic and international competition.

6. Sixth: There are weaknesses and new problems being faced by the Japanese QC circle movement.

The QC circle is no panacea! Based on the Japanese experience, there are problems that must be dealt with. And, I think these are not often understood in the United States.

First of all, the real value of the QC circle lies in the principle of voluntary participation on the part of workers. This means that the individual QC circle does not function well if some members participate and some do not. There are two situations in which the members do not want to participate. One is where the worker lacks the ability to assume an active role in the QC circle. Worker training is extremely important here. The other situation is more complicated. There are some workers who do not like circle activities, in part because of different personalities and value systems. There are some, especially young workers, who are more leisure oriented. Under current circumstances, these workers may feel a subtle but coercive pressure from management, resulting from an atmosphere of tacit understanding that every worker should be a circle member. When this occurs, there is a lack of spontaneity, the circle activities are not very productive, and circles often become inactive.

Second, in principle QC circle activities must be autonomous. However, foremen and/or quality control engineering staff need to be involved in directing, training, and advising in QC techniques. As a result of this involvement some workers may feel manipulated by management. In a word, it is difficult to create among the workers the true feeling that "I participate in the circle voluntarily and play a role in it autonomously."

Third, since the QC circle is voluntary by nature, it is not desirable to assess the degree of individual worker contribution in a performance appraisal. However, management must recognize individual worker contribution in order to encourage further development of QC activity. This is yet another management dilemma.

These problems are not peculiar to the auto industry. They are commonly observed in all Japanese industries that have QC circles. Moreover, as a result of almost twenty years' experience with QC circles, some new problems are emerging. Some workers are now dissatisfied with circle activities because they find them ritualistic and mere formalities. They find nothing new in what they are doing. Management is finding it more and more difficult to attract workers to circle activity. More and more workers are just going through the motions simply to "keep management off their backs."

Also, workers are finding it increasingly difficult to identify new problems to solve. And some workers are critical of management's not giving enough assistance while at the same time expecting too much in the way of results from the employee.

Compensation for the time spent on QC circle activity is another complicated problem. To have circle activities during the normal working hour is desirable. But there are departments such as assembly lines and operations where it is impossible to do so. In this case, circle activities are held outside the normal working hours. If the time spent on circle activities is paid without any restriction, these activities will become the means for workers to earn additional overtime income. If not paid at all, workers will lose any monetary incentive.

Toyota pays for all hours spent on the circle activities. Honda does not. Initially, Honda paid for overtime but changed several years ago to a no-payment policy in order to make the QC circle activities really voluntary and autonomous. Nissan has a practice of paying for a limit of two hours a month in principle, but it pays for all hours when the company recognizes the extra circle activities as necessary or inevitable. In cases where time spent on the QC circle activities is not fully paid, the rank-and-file workers are pushing their unions to negotiate with the companies to pay more.

There is another problem related to the economic situation. The best time to introduce QC circles smoothly is when the economic growth is high and wage increases are high. It is more difficult to introduce QC circles and operate them successfully when economic growth is low and wage increases are smaller. It is now the spring wage offensive time in Japan. Japanese union leaders are taking very strong positions against company managements in wage negotiations this year. Their policy is to get a full share of the "pie" being produced by QC circle activities. This is because we have a situation where increases in wages and bonuses are getting smaller as a result of the slower growth rate of the economy as a whole. In the auto industry, production actually fell during 1981 for the major automobile manufacturers.

Demographic factors are also creating problems. Older workers are increasing in absolute numbers. This is a result of both the relative aging of the labor force and an extension of the compulsory retirement age. In this context, the seniority wage system has an adverse effect on management. The typically passive role of older workers in QC circles will probably have an adverse effect on circle activity. Increasing tax rates and social insurance premiums for workers as well as corporations may also reduce incentives.

While the impact of new technology is not yet known, some management and union personnel fear that robots and other numerical control machines will limit opportunities for participatory work practices in Japan. With the introduction of robots, Japanese auto companies are, on the one hand, increasing profits by saving labor. On the other hand, however, such steps could lead to a collapse of the total teamwork system found in Japanese industry.

Finally, I would like to close with the following observation: throughout the postwar period and in many respects throughout the history of Japanese industrialization, Japanese management and workers have been spurred by a sense of crisis. In the case of the auto industry, there has been a succession of such crises in recent years—from the trade liberalization period of the mid-1960s to the "Oil Shocks" of 1973 and 1979. Throughout these periods, the industry's goal has been to compete with and catch up to the leading automotive manufacturers in the United States in both productivity and quality. The motivation for the kinds of participatory activities about which I have spoken must be understood in this light. Nowadays, since the Japanese have achieved a position as the world's number one manufacturer of cars and trucks, there is a feeling among not a few Japanese workers that further improvements in productivity and quality will only lead to more serious trade problems with the United States. To put this in American terms, we Japanese may be losing our "number two, we try harder" mentality, and therefore incentives for further improvement may be declining. In this context, I do earnestly hope that the strength of the American auto industry will be renewed so that auto manufacturers in the two countries can maintain a healthy competitive relationship. Thank you very much.

THE "JUST-IN-TIME" SYSTEM:
ITS RELEVANCE FOR THE U. S. AUTO INDUSTRY

Robert B. Stone

As you know, things haven't been going that well for the U. S. auto industry for the past two years or so. In fact, the theme of this conference, "The Industry at the Crossroads," is certainly appropriate. The industry is in trouble and must find ways to become more competitive.

General Motors is no exception. We must find ways to cut costs too—and we're examining every avenue that will lead to more efficient, cost-effective, competitive operations.

As far as General Motors is concerned, we lost one opportunity when we failed to come to an agreement with the UAW on ways to decrease the labor cost differential at the end of January. However, as you know, we resumed talks just yesterday and our hopes are high that we will reach an agreement.

But I'm not going to dwell on labor cost differences. We must also continue looking for *other* opportunities—other ways to become more competitive. This is our most compelling challenge.

One thing we're going to have to do in the purchasing end of the business is to make better use of our make-or-buy process to reach decisions. This, of course, will likely result in more outsourcing for us. We *must* sort out the best places to get things done—to buy materials and components at the most competitive cost—be that manufacturers outside of General Motors or manufacturers outside of the country.

Another thing we are looking at to help us get more competitive is applications of Just-in-Time inventory control systems. That's where I'd like to concentrate our thoughts and cover our plans with you at today's conference. Japanese

Robert B. Stone is Vice President in charge of Materials Management, General Motors Corporation. Art work for the figures in this article was supplied by the General Motors Photographic section.

manufacturers, through just such techniques as Kanban, have truly effective inventory management and production control.

Very simply, the Just-in-Time (Kanban) system provides that only the right parts in the right quantity are produced at the right time.

Scheduling in the auto industry involves communicating to all production processes the timing and quantity of parts required. U. S. auto companies develop parts shipping schedules by exploding (breaking down and itemizing) the forecasted vehicle assembly schedule to part numbers. Then they communicate these schedules to all their suppliers. These suppliers, in turn, develop their own production schedules and explode these schedules into parts shipping schedules which then are communicated to their own suppliers. These steps are repeated for as many supply levels as exist. Generally, each supply level requires one week to develop its own production schedule and communicate it to the next downstream supply process. This system is relatively inflexible, and to compensate for the time required to communicate changes, significant inventories are maintained.

The Japanese Just-in-Time system is a reverse method from that employed by U. S. auto companies. Only the vehicle final assembly lines accurately know the timing and quantity of parts required. Thus the final assembly line goes to its suppliers and brings back the necessary parts at the necessary time for vehicle assembly. These suppliers then produce exactly the kind and quantity of parts to replace those taken by the assembly line. To produce these parts, these suppliers go to their own suppliers and get only the necessary parts. In this fashion, the entire supply chain reacts quickly to actual vehicle assembly, and Just-in-Time production is achieved.

I have described how the actual flow of material is controlled. In addition, there is a planning system which communicates to all suppliers, in advance, the approximate daily requirements for the next three months. It is crucial to the proper functioning of a Just-in-Time system that actual final assembly not deviate from these plans by more than 20 percent during the first month of the plan. The Japanese have also been successful in attaining relative stability of schedules up to this time.

The preceding was a conceptual description of the Japanese Just-in-Time system. The usual implementation involves the assembly lines and all other user processes keeping a relatively small inventory of all the parts they use. Attached to each container of parts is a card. When they start to use a container, the card is removed and sent to the supplier. This supplier then sends a replacement container of that part number with the card attached to it and in turn produces one container of that part number to replace what has been taken.

Another way to view it is that the U. S. auto industry pushes material through the pipeline in accordance with schedules based on forecast assembly. The Japanese Just-in-Time approach is to pull material through the pipeline based on what is actually built.

There are several requirements for Just-in-Time systems to work most effectively.

First is geographic concentration. Relatively short transit times—less than a day—are necessary if the using process is to bring back the parts it requires Just-in-Time. The Japanese auto industry, including most suppliers, is clustered around three cities—Tokyo, Nagoya, and Hiroshima, as shown in Figure 1. Toyota, for example, has most of its suppliers located within 60 miles of its plants. Contrast that situation with General Motors, where we have assembly plants, represented by the dots in Figure 2, scattered all over the United States and Canada. Note also though that most suppliers and many assembly plants are clustered in the midwest as shown by the shaded area. For these operations we believe Just-in-Time can work.

The second requirement is dependable quality. The using process must always be able to rely on receiving only good parts from its suppliers. The Japanese concept is that every operation must regard the next operation as the ultimate customer, and pass only perfect products along. *To do this, quality control efforts are focused on controlling the production process, not on inspection, to weed out the bad.* We are working with Dr. Deming and others to expand the use of statistical quality control methods to improve our manufacturing quality.

The third is a manageable supplier network. Most Japanese auto companies use fewer than 250 parts suppliers. By contrast, General Motors uses about 3,500 suppliers for our assembly operations alone.[1] The complexity of communications is obvious. We are reviewing our current supplier policies and intend to reduce and simplify our entire supplier network. We are also planning to shift to long-term relationships with many of our suppliers and have already begun to involve some key suppliers in the development of our new products at the earliest stage.

The fourth requirement is a controlled transportation system with short, reliable transit times. Japanese auto companies use only dedicated (single-purpose) trucks to ship parts, and deliveries occur several times a day from each supplier at prescheduled times. Our normal mode for most shipments has been rail, which involves frequent delays in switching yards. We have changed many of our shorter moves to truck during the last year—frequently resulting in a freight

1. General Motors has more than 30,000 suppliers providing production material machinery, tooling, and services. The 3,500 refers to parts suppliers who service General Motors' assembly operations.

Figure 1

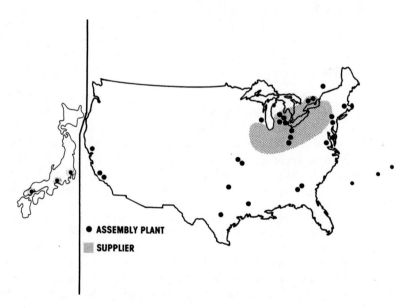

Figure 2

saving, as well as inventory reduction—and we are building our new plants with the capability of handling more than 300 truck deliveries per day.

Fifth is manufacturing flexibility so that the supplying process can react quickly to produce the parts taken by the using process. This translates into fast die/tool changes. The accomplishments of the Japanese have been well publicized. For example, automated press lines changed in under six minutes, injection molding machines changed in less than two minutes. This is an area in which we are struggling with only limited success to date. One of our plastics plants has been able to reduce its mold change time from about ninety minutes to under fifteen minutes. Traditionally, U. S. industry has accepted changeover time as a given and the concept of Economic Order Quantity (EOQ) has been used to balance the trade-off between inventory cost and changeover cost. The Just-in-Time system throws out the EOQ concept and forces reduction in changeover time.

Sixth is small lot size. Most Japanese companies employing Just-in-Time systems require lot size to be less than 10 percent of a day's usage. This is necessary so that supplying processes quickly react to produce what has been taken by the using process. The Japanese ideal is to achieve a lot size of one piece so that every time one vehicle is produced, one of each part in the vehicle is also produced.

Seventh is efficient receiving and material-handling procedures. Most Japanese companies have eliminated formal receiving operations. Whole sides of plants act as receiving areas, and parts are delivered as close as possible to the point of use. The kinds of trucks used eliminate the need for truck wells, and delivery to lineside is expedited.

Last, and perhaps most important, is strong management commitment to making a Just-in-Time system work. Incentives must frequently be changed, as I will illustrate in a moment with one of our own experiences. The resources necessary to reduce changeover times and to improve the production processes must be made available. Management must continuously prod the entire organization to seek improvement. And during the conversion period—when it will seem like the world's falling apart—management must maintain the resolve to see the program through. (See Figure 3.)

Notice that I did not mention product simplicity as a requirement. Contrary to the belief of many Americans, we judge the Japanese product offering, when viewed from the materials management perspective, to be approximately the same as ours. Toyota, for example, produces fifteen carlines using eighteen different engines. Most are produced in both left-hand and right-hand drive. In their Takaoka plant, Toyota assembles, on one line, the rear-wheel-drive Corolla and the front-wheel-drive Tercel in both left- and right-hand drive.

REQUIREMENTS FOR JUST-IN-TIME

1. **GEOGRAPHIC CONCENTRATION**
2. **DEPENDABLE QUALITY**
3. **MANAGEABLE SUPPLIER NETWORK**
4. **CONTROLLED TRANSPORTATION SYSTEM**
5. **MANUFACTURING FLEXIBILITY**
6. **SMALL LOT SIZES**
7. **EFFICIENT RECEIVING & MATERIAL HANDLING**
8. **MANAGEMENT COMMITMENT**

Figure 3

INVENTORY/RIVER ANALOGY

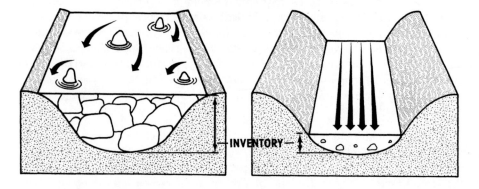

Figure 4

Why a Just-in-Time system? Our prime motivation is to reduce inventory to free up capital for use elsewhere in the business. General Motors alone has about nine billion dollars tied up in inventory. It appears that the entire Japanese auto industry gets by with considerably less. But to the Japanese, the real motivation is to force productivity improvement. Our early experience bears this out.

The Japanese use an analogy that compares a production process to a river with many stagnant pools (see Figure 4). The flow of water is analogous to the flow of material. The level of water is analogous to the size of inventory. The bottom of the river is strewn with boulders of various sizes, which interfere with the smooth flow. These are analogous to the problems inherent in any production process. If the level of water in the river is lowered a little, the largest boulders will surface and can be removed to smooth the flow of water. Subsequent further lowerings will reveal progressively smaller boulders which can also be removed. The final result, then, will be a swiftly flowing stream. In the same way, as inventory in a production process is lowered, the major problems in that process will become apparent, and the entire organization can—and must—dedicate the resources necessary to solve that problem. The result of solving these problems is improved productivity.

An added benefit of Just-in-Time systems as implemented by the Japanese is a reduction in computers and people required to support the production process. In the Japanese world there are no inventory records for parts, and no expediters to follow shipments.

Now I'd like to turn to some of our experiences in trying to adopt, and adapt, Just-in-Time systems.

Our major success to date has been achieved with high-cost components. Our Michigan assembly plants determine their requirement for the next day for engines, axles, transmissions, frames, and a few other commodities. These are then telephoned to the suppliers in the morning, and just those requirements are shipped, by truck, that afternoon/evening to support the next day's production. Our previous practice was to determine an average daily requirement based on the week's forecasted schedule and to ship accordingly, but actual production by day deviated significantly from the forecasted daily average. This telephone program has been very successful, not only in inventory reduction but also as a learning experience. Many of our component divisions have also started similar programs for the high value material supplied to them.

We have also just started a pilot program involving our Linden, New Jersey, and Tarrytown, New York, plants—extending this concept to a broader range of commodities and more suppliers, including some outside suppliers. Here we are dealing with longer transit times so the assembly plants are determining their requirements out as far as five days. It is too soon to know the results from this pilot, but we're convinced this is the way to go for our assembly plants outside the midwest, and we expect inventory reductions of over 100 million dollars from this program.

Our only failure to date came in a situation where we failed to address the incentives. We have a daily efficiency system in most of our operations which measures the labor content of the parts produced against the actual labor used to produce them. In one of our plants we implemented a Just-in-Time system for one department, using cards just like the Japanese do. In-process inventory was reduced 75 percent, problems were getting recognized and solved, and the materials management people at the plant judged it a success and wanted to expand it plant-wide. However, the production superintendent could not accept turning off his equipment when no production was required. This was contrary to the incentive we provided him, to be efficient on a daily basis.

This experience points out a major stumbling block we must overcome if we are to make Just-in-Time work for us. U. S. industry has a profit-center orientation that frequently results in suboptimization of the total process. At General Motors, with our decentralized approach, we sometimes act like different teams in one league rather than a group of players on the same team. Just-in-Time requires a greater degree of coordination than our traditional methods. To be successful we must address and solve the organization and incentive problems.

We are now starting Just-in-Time systems in three of our engine plants. This time we've done a lot of ground work in installing statistical quality control methods, getting employee involvement, and reducing inventories to minimum levels. We're hopeful that these will be successful and will serve as a spring board for our other manufacturing operations.

I've described our experiences to date. We're really only at the threshold, and it's taken nearly three years to get this far. Why such slow progress?

In an industry as large as the U. S. auto industry, particularly one which had been so successful, there is tremendous inertia. The same is true at General Motors. It took us more than a year to accept that the Japanese were beating us in the area of materials management. It took another year for our people to accept the notion that less inventory would be a good thing. We still don't have widespread acceptance of our ability to make Just-in-Time work, but we are making progress. I wish I could give you the magic formula, but one doesn't exist. Progress is agonizingly slow. But unless we, the entire auto industry, begin, the task will never be done.

LEARNING FROM THE JAPANESE?

Robert E. Cole

We have begun this past Fall a new research project at the University of Michigan, sponsored by U. S. and Japanese auto firms and including the UAW. We are examining major developments in the respective auto industries and the prospects for mutual prosperity. That project, along with my own research, has allowed me the opportunity to reflect a great deal on this issue of what we can learn from the Japanese. In my judgment there is an awful lot of nonsense being written on the subject, but some good things as well. We must learn to separate the wheat from the chaff. There are also some lessons which are being overlooked. We tend to concentrate on techniques instead of the broader lessons involving alternative approaches to management. I was at a plant recently where management wanted to adopt Japanese-style participatory practices. I listened to the top management team spend a half hour discussing whether to have workers do exercises every morning before work, Japanese style. They had totally missed the point. The point is participation—to let the workers decide if they want to do exercises. If the objective is more participation, then there are lots of vehicles through which that can be accomplished. Quality circles, the current vogue, is only one of the many vehicles. Here I am in full agreement with Professor Fujita. The point is to focus on developing a process, not to concentrate on a single technique as a magic key.

The Japanese certainly got our attention with the tremendous surge in competitive power of their exports. In industry after industry, they have successfully challenged us in our foreign and domestic markets. Naturally we began to ask what was the basis for their success. Moreover, the journalists began pointing to the Japanese companies' alleged success in operating manufacturing plants in the United States with U. S. workers—much of which is overblown in my judgment. Existing explanations for the Japanese success, like low wages, strong work ethic, unique culture, and close cooperation between industry and government

Robert E. Cole is Professor of Sociology at The University of Michigan and U. S. Project Director for the Joint U. S.-Japan Automotive Study.

were recognized increasingly as inadequate. Attention became focused on their management style, and properly so in my judgement. Scholars and journalists began to churn out detailed explanations of Japanese success. It's their quality circles, it's their Just-in-Time system, and so on.

With all this we are now starting to see a reaction. Managers and workers are getting tired of being told how the Japanese do everything better. A number of exaggerated claims have been called into question. While there are many who would learn from Japan, it is also true that interested parties often select out of the Japanese experience what serves their narrow interests and then use it to beat the heads of their opponents. Management, labor, and government people all play this game. The manufacturers often use it against suppliers, and so on. Unfortunately, in this scenario, learning often takes second place to scoring points.

As the reaction sets in, a number of people are starting to say, let's forget about the Japanese. All we need to do is roll up our sleeves, rely on good old American know-how, and get the job done. Furthermore, the Japanese are only doing what we taught them in the first place! In effect they are saying: "We have taken our three-week Japanese plant tour. We talked to our Japanese supplier or our OEM, we've read *Theory Z*, so we know all we need to know." In this fashion, one-shot reports replace continuous learning and stereotypes replace understanding.

Now the Japanese have been studying and learning from us for over 100 years. Though they now believe they have less to learn from us, they still continue to monitor closely U. S. developments in technology and management practices and strategies. *Now that is a lesson worth learning!* They map their external environment extremely well.

No doubt the current Japanese fad will fade, but clearly the Japanese competitive threat will not go away. We need to stay open to examining options and alternatives to current practices. One of their great strengths is their openness to new ideas, especially foreign ideas. They don't have a "not invented here" syndrome. They believe a good idea is a good idea no matter where it came from. We need this same openness if we are to remain competitive. And we still know precious little about how Japanese industry operates, in my judgment. How many people in the American auto industry really understand how the Just-in-Time system operates from a supplier perspective? Do we really understand the Japanese approach to quality? A lot of industry people are already starting to become complacent because we seem to be making some big strides in improving auto quality. But this improvement can be deceptive. It is always easier to improve product quality in an economic downturn as old plants are closed and inexperienced workers laid off. In addition, it is easier to send parts back to suppliers under slack conditions. The real test is what happens when production picks up.

We have yet to put new incentive systems in place. In short, we have no basis for being complacent. There is still a lot of hard work which needs to be done, and that includes studying Japanese practices on a continuous basis.

I want to discuss briefly what is involved in the process of borrowing across societies. To make my point, let me highlight a statement made by Professor Fujita which absolutely violates all the conventional wisdom we have about participatory practices in Japanese industry. He argues that participatory practices succeeded *in spite* of Japanese culture, not because of it. They succeeded because of a sustained and tenacious strategy on the part of Japanese management to make it work. Now, if he is right, and I believe there is a lot of truth to the argument, it has enormous implications for the borrowing process. It means that the Japanese do not have an inate advantage over us in the use of participatory work practices as many believe. It also means that a sustained and tenacious commitment on the part of management and other relevant parties—i.e., the unions and the workers themselves—can bring about the institutionalization of these practices. Unfortunately, I see situations in which top management and top union leadership in the United States give lip service to such innovations but have only superficial knowledge and are really not prepared to make the kinds of organizational changes necessary for participatory practices to take hold.

What kinds of changes am I talking about? Let me just provide one example, but I think it is a profound one. Japanese auto management shares information with blue collar workers that we don't often share with first- and second-line supervisors: budget information, cost information, warranty data, etc. That information has been vital for making the problem-solving activities of small groups successful in Japan. Now, who makes the decision to release such information? Certainly not the quality-of-work-life coordinator in a plant or first- and second-line supervisors, and sometimes not even the plant manager. That is a top management decision, and until those kinds of decisions start to get made, we will not see the institutionalization of these kinds of practices in U. S. firms. It will be just one more program "down the pike." Incidentally, such sharing is happening in some plants, such as Chevrolet Gear and Axle. But this is still the exception, not the rule.

While on this subject of information, let me add the following observation with regard to a lesson offered by the Japanese. When it comes to controlling the production process, the Japanese are very selective about the kinds of information they collect. And they keep things simple. We saw that in Mr. Stone's description of the Just-in-Time system. If one was to measure level of industrial *strength* by the degree of sophistication in internal information systems, we would be far and away number one, and the Japanese would be number ten, or something of that order. That suggests to me that we ought to do some rethinking here. Maybe American business schools ought to take the lead since they bear some responsibility for getting us into the bind in the first place. Measurement and information systems are primarily designed to monitor the firm's performance in a variety of areas and thereby help control the direction of activities. They should serve as problem-solving tools, but in practice, many U. S. firms have developed overly elaborated measurement systems which have turned into powerful control mechanisms. These serve primarily to distribute rewards and punishments. In the process, information not only loses its utility for problem solving but it comes to hinder the problem-solving process. Risk taking is discouraged. The driving force here may be our obsession with frequent management appraisals and lack of willingness to allow employees discretion in doing their jobs. It needs to be reassessed. The broader issue is the delicate balance between the use of information for control and for problem solving.

It is obvious by now that we are not talking about copying the Japanese. We need only look at what the Japanese did when borrowing from us. They often took things out of context—totally ripping them from their social nexus—and adapted them to their own uses. That violates our common sense understanding. There was also a lot of what one Japanese speaker here last year called creative misunderstanding. They misunderstood what they saw, but in the process of borrowing they created something new, and it was something new which worked. And lest anyone doubt it, they displayed great creative capacities in the process. Contrary to some of our stereotypes, borrowing is a very creative act, especially when you are dealing with organizational technologies. There is no reason to think we are any less creative than the Japanese in this regard.

RESPONSES OF CONFERENCE PANELISTS
TO AUDIENCE QUESTIONS

Panelists for the afternoon question and answer session were William J. ABERNATHY, Professor in the School of Business Administration, Harvard University; Robert E. COLE, Professor of Sociology, The University of Michigan; Yoshitaka FUJITA, Professor, the Faculty of Economics, Asia University, Tokyo; and Robert B. STONE, Vice President for Materials Management, General Motors Corporation. The moderator was Fred SECREST, Consultant and former Executive Vice President, Ford Motor Company.

Q: The General Motors approach to inventory management seems to stress the transportation factor—the effectiveness of close geographical relationship between suppliers and assembly plants. To what extent do you believe this factor will affect future sourcing decisions in the U. S. industry in terms of changing the geographical location of suppliers?

STONE: I'm concerned sometimes that people may think General Motors intends to eliminate suppliers from particular regions or to begin to use only a handful of suppliers, and I'd like to clear that up as best I can. The U. S. auto industry will be reducing its supplier base; we will use direct suppliers and negotiate more closely with them. We will have more long-term agreements with suppliers than we've had in the past. This is not going to happen right away, and it doesn't mean that big suppliers are more advantageously placed than small ones. But a supplier using statistical quality control methods to assure uniform quality parts will have a front line with General Motors and other companies who adopt these new inventory systems, there isn't any question about that. This doesn't throw out pricing and delivery as considerations in our choice of suppliers, but quality has become very important and is a needed item in a supplier's profile.

Q: To what extent is the alleged insistence of U. S. auto industry management for exhaustive—at times almost redundant—data and reporting before they are willing to take action a contributing factor in the industry's problems? Is there a significant difference in the data bases or the degree of reporting required by the management of Japanese and American factories?

ABERNATHY: I'm not really an authority on that, although I was struck by the fact that the Japanese typewriter, with its hundreds of characters, was too cumbersome to use extensively for internal communications. I had a sense during my tour that there was a lot less written communication in Japanese firms. This of course is very natural, since their business relationships are usually longer term, there's less job turnover and position switching, the timing grade is longer— and there's more interdepartmental trust. All these can give them a significant productivity advantage.

I think that data base management is indeed a problem in the United States. Much of it is done to accommodate ignorance, so that somebody who doesn't know a lot about the specific production questions has data sufficient to make decisions. The problem is not nearly as acute in the auto firms as it would be in conglomerates and other firms like General Electric which have very diverse product lines; in those cases top management can't possibly know everything about the business and needs much more information to operate.

Q: No one today has placed much emphasis on the differing extent to which robotics are used in Japanese and American auto industries. What is the relative impact of robots in the two countries, and what may develop in the future?

FUJITA: Japan is frequently mentioned nowadays for its extensive introduction of robotics and office automation. In the auto industry, however, these technical innovations have been applied in only limited areas—particularly in "dirty" jobs. Robots have been introduced in larger numbers in some other Japanese industries like the chemical, electrical, and machinery industries. The impact of the new technology is not yet known, although some management and union leaders fear that robots and other production machinery will replace the emphasis on people involvement in achieving productivity and quality improvements. Introducing robots increases the profits of Japanese auto companies by saving labor costs, but it could have negative effects on the production system as a whole.

Q: There seems to be some disagreement about how truly voluntary the Japanese quality control circle approach is. Would you comment on that?

COLE: In principle, the quality circles in Japan are voluntary; all the Japanese literature on the subject stresses that. In practice, however, it is known that there is tremendous variation among companies and industries in how voluntary those activities are; in most companies with circles, there is strong pressure on all workers to belong to quality circles. Not to do so would suggest to management a lack of commitment to corporate goals and thereby damage one's promotion prospects. There are companies that have quota systems—so many suggestions per circle, so many suggestions per month—which are hardly models of voluntarism. Everything is relative though; one Japanese official said to me not long ago, "Well, if you think ours aren't voluntary, look at the Korean circles."

The principle of voluntarism is a more powerful one in our society, both by virtue of the values our workers hold and because our unions are stronger. This may be a potential advantage we have over the Japanese. Japanese experts suggest that the more voluntary the activities, the more effective circles are in the long run. If that's true, and we can succeed in establishing quality circles or other small-scale participatory activities with a high degree of voluntarism, we may realize this long-term advantage.

Q: As the Japanese build plants in this country—the Japanese auto companies are beginning to follow the lead of their television, motorcycle, and some other businesses—are the inventory control, quality circle, and other participatory systems they have developed likely to be successfully exported by Japanese management to their American production facilities?

ABERNATHY: I visited the U. S. plant of one Japanese firm recently and talked to the new American plant manager. He was swearing at the facilities designers in Tokyo, saying, "Don't those dummies there understand that we have snow on the road here, and that our suppliers are 400 miles away, and we have trucking strikes and traffic jams, and that there's no room here for parts inventory." He had been struggling with the design people in Japan, trying to get them to understand that there was a need in the United States for a significant level of inventory—unless they were willing to buy up a whole state and turn it into an industrial infrastructure of one sort or another.

I suspect that some of the larger inventories maintained by U. S. manufacturers is there for very good reasons: this is a big country and we do have uncertain transportation systems. Over the long run I would expect to see Japanese inventories rise a little bit and ours go down a little bit as we discover that some of it is unnecessary. I believe that Japanese-owned plants in this country will require more inventory than those in Japan.

Regionalism is a real problem for several reasons in the auto industry. Volkswagen learned this in 1973, for as the Bug went out of style, there was a lot of gnashing of teeth in Wolfsburg—the whole region where Volkswagen had concentrated its manufacturing was badly affected. Another lesson was learned in 1914 when the entire auto industry was concentrated in Detroit and put a terrific strain on the nation's railroad system—actually tying up much of it at one point—trying to ship out cars to all parts of the country. A third reason is that industrial dispersion has significant advantages for national defense—otherwise one well-placed bomb could take out an entire industry without much difficulty.

COLE: My experience in visiting a variety of Japanese-managed plants in the United States is that, contrary to the popular view, very few of them have quality circles. It turns out that the Japanese managers are extremely conservative; they're feeling their way, they don't know how to deal with the multiethnic labor force or with U.S. unions. In general, I find the press reports about Japanese firms in the United States are extraordinarily distorted. The public relations departments of these firms like to pass out a cheerful message, but the message bears little relation to the reality.

Q: Doesn't the Just-in-Time system, as practiced by General Motors, simply transfer the inventory problem to the supplier? Aren't there additional levels of sophistication and communication necessary in order to achieve the advantages of the system for all the participants in the materials chain?

STONE: It should not result in transferring inventory to the supplier. The goal is to reduce inventory at every level of the supply process. It definitely sets up a different sort of manufacturer-supplier relationship. The materials system that we're moving to needs, and will always need, a planning or forecasting system that will let our whole network of suppliers—our own General Motors plants that feed our assembly lines as well as outside suppliers—know what our production plans are. Beyond that, however, all operations will have new responsibilities to plan production without always waiting for someone to tell them what to do next. The feeder plants particularly will need to be able to react more quickly than they do now. The old procedure of running a thirty-day supply—"make sure you tell me far enough in advance so I can run thirty days"—may change a great deal. If that is what is meant by pushing some responsibility back to the suppliers, then it is inherent in the new system and is very much needed.

Q: The quality control circles and some of the other manager-worker involvement programs that we've heard about have been used in Japanese industries for at least twenty years. We've also heard that Japanese industries are changing, that the work force is changing, and that the stable growth rate in the auto industry is probably beginning to slow down. Is the number of employees involved in circles and other participatory programs still growing, and are employees and managers still equally involved and motivated in mature Japanese industries?

FUJITA: The idea of quality control circles was imported from the United States—many of their procedures were developed and applied in the U. S. space program—but their use is still growing in Japan. As of 1980 there were one million registered members in Japanese quality control associations, and it's estimated that there are about ten million quality control circle members—one in every three workers—in Japan. The rate of increase in the last two decades is beginning to level off.

There is a wide belief among managers and workers that if companies and workers introduce quality control circles they will survive the present high levels of competition, and that if they don't they may face bankruptcy and unemployment. It's my opinion that more quality control circles or similar activities will be introduced. Workers are learning more about production problems, and management people—including engineers and top management—are feeling the pressure to keep up their own quality study efforts.

COLE: My own reading of participation in quality circles is that membership is more on the order of one in eight workers rather than one in three. It serves a lot of people's and organizations' purposes to exaggerate the number. Nonetheless, participation is of major significance and growing, particularly in the service sector. On the other hand, in some mature process industries like chemicals, reliance on circle activities has declined over the last decade.

Q: To what extent does the difference in the educational qualifications of American and Japanese auto workers play a part in the ability of Japanese industries to make participatory and quality control activities function so effectively? Some of us have heard that the Japanese companies with lifetime or quasi-lifetime employment practices tend to get the pick of the high school graduates, and that they therefore have a better-trained work force to start with.

COLE: First, I don't think that working in an automobile company is necessarily the most desirable job in Japan, or in the United States, particularly for blue-collar workers. During the labor shortage of the early 1970s, the auto firms had a lot of difficulty recruiting blue-collar workers. Toyota may be an exception: they're located in a rural area where they have been the premier employer, paying higher than the prevailing wage, and working for them has been seen as a very secure and desirable position. There's no doubt that there is a certain homogeneity and standardization of the educational product in Japan. They have a highly centralized education system, and it means that the quality is pretty uniform; it's also quite high. On UNESCO tests of math and science skills, Japanese students consistently rank at the very top. In the science tests, Japan ranked first and the United States fifteenth out of nineteen countries. These are not just college-bound students by the way, but regular high school students. This would appear to give the Japanese a significant advantage. For example, many of the statistical techniques used in quality circles are part of the Japanese high school curriculum.

ABERNATHY: The education question is deeply disturbing to me, and I certainly agree with everything Bob Cole said. But I think it's important to understand how serious it is. Historically, the United States has always had the highest standard of education for our young people of any country in the world. We always have had the highest wage rates and the highest percentage of the basic population going through school. Various European investigations of the U.S. economy, from the nineteenth century on, have concluded that the strength of our manufacturing system was the quality and educational level of our work force. That our advantage here has disappeared means, I think, that the United States is becoming more like England, where education for the elite in the big schools may be better than anybody's, but that the average education offered is absolutely lousy. I know that calling for increased attention to education sounds like a soapbox plea, but in many ways the source of growth, productivity, and rising living standards in the United States has been our broadly based educational system.

FUJITA: In Japan, in a given age group, approximately 95 percent will have been graduated from senior high school, and 38 percent have attended college. The first figure is higher than that of the United States, but the second proportion is lower than yours. We consider your level of average education superior. Moreover, more educated workers are not necessarily better; some Japanese use their education to make better excuses for not working harder. But there is a fever for education among Japanese children: many youngsters forgo summer vacation and study in after-school programs to improve their work skills. The strong pressure in the educational system in Japan has taught discipline to young workers in the past, and as more Japanese grow up "rich," without the practical financial pressures for educational achievement, the effects on work force discipline are unpredictable.

COLE: I'd like to make a few further comments. In recent eighteen-year-old cohorts, as Professor Fujita said, about 95 percent of the Japanese graduate from high school; the proportion in the United States is about 87 percent. True, more people in the United States begin college, but since our college drop-out rate is considerably higher, in the early twenties-age cohorts Japan now has as high a percentage of college graduates as we do.

I agree that we should distinguish between quantity and quality of education. I don't think there's any doubt that the elementary and secondary school systems in Japan produce better and more uniformly educated students than we do, although not without considerable cost. Talking with Japanese intellectuals, particularly if they have teenage children, about their major dissatisfactions with Japanese society quickly leads to the topic of the education system. It causes great pain in many families—five-year-old children taking tests to get into certain kindergartens, and if they fail, they've lost the opportunity to proceed up a particular education ladder. This is an incredible thing to see. In general, I think the quality of American universities is superior to that of Japanese universities, and more gets done in our universities than gets done in Japanese universities. But at the secondary level they do a hell of a job.

Q: We've heard that sometimes the Just-in-Time inventory system hasn't worked in U. S. plants because the incentive system as perceived by the plant management was in conflict with some of the essentials involved in the new inventory approach. Could you elaborate on this and discuss alternative incentives that the corporation management has found useful?

STONE: Whether you are a production foreman, a department foreman, a production superintendent overseeing half the plant, or the plant manager, there are many characterisitics of the job and your performance that vie with one another for top priority, and these must be balanced somehow. If you are a foreman with 20 or 100 people under you, they are going to work eight hours a day whatever your responsibilities. At General Motors there's a standard hour routing that pays so many hours per hundred or per thousand parts flowing through your department on a standard cost basis. If you pass through a hundred standard hours of output in a hundred hours of time, you've got 100 percent efficiency. Achieving that efficiency is very important if you work for General Motors.

Now suddenly we're introducing that foreman to a different measurement of his work; we want him now to run only what is needed, which allows him to take some of his work force, according to his own criteria, and use them on other jobs. We want only a certain number of parts coming through the system. We've given him a new goal: no inventory. He's not even going to get the stock to start production if it isn't necessary. Clearly this can conflict with the daily efficiency system. General Motors is trying to make less inventory one of the prime incentives for all of our production processes. And we are trying to demonstrate to our production managers, by many examples, that quality and full utilization of machines and facilities will result from achieving this new goal.

Q: How well do you think the Japanese quality circle approach will work and is working with American workers and American management?

FUJITA: Again, I would like to emphasize that quality circles were an American invention, and there is no special reason to believe that they cannot be successful here. Individual workers in the United States tend to be more competitive than their Japanese counterparts. The problem for U. S. personnel management is to find efficient systems for channeling this competitiveness—to make workers and management cooperate more closely and creatively. When I visited General Motors and Ford factories twenty years ago, I was surprised to see how hard the American workers worked—especially in comparison to the Japanese at that time. I praised the hard-working attitude of American workers in a book I wrote, and I wouldn't mind seeing my argument proven true again today.

Q: If the "world car" programs involve not so much the production of identical cars from scratch in many countries but some degree of component design commonality (which will necessitate some foreign sourcing—in some cases also to meet local-content laws), will these programs conflict with the requirements of the "close-to-zero" inventory systems also being introduced?

STONE: I don't think the two are completely incompatible. The world car concept isn't as total as it was originally talked about several years ago. A T-car in Germany, a T-car in Brazil, and a T-car in the United States are all very similar, but they aren't identical; as the questioner observed, that isn't what is meant by a world car. But with respect to components—especially in the power train—if production facilities can be maximally utilized by producing major parts (say a transmission module) in one country and shipping them to other countries, these are workable world car procedures. Now scheduling this kind of production, involving trans-oceanic transport, is manageable, and can be compatible with Just-in-Time inventory control. But the procedures will clearly be different from those involved in manufacturing cars from parts made within a fifty-mile radius of the assembly plant.

SECREST: Some questioners have also wondered about whether the new labor agreements will effect out-sourcing or other sourcing decisions associated with further applications of these new inventory policies. I suspect this will also involve pragmatic case-by-case evaluation. It may be that sourcing decisions over the next two or three years under the new automotive contracts will involve a different degree of evaluation of work force relations. But to some extent that has always been the case.

Q: In your judgment, is the power of the UAW in the automobile companies and the major auto suppliers a serious impediment to the adoption by American management and workers of the best of the Japanese methods? Or is it a neutral or beneficial factor?

ABERNATHY: It seems to me that the UAW is one of the most progressive and forward-looking labor organizations in the country. When I think about the crisis facing the U. S. auto industry, it appears that the flexibility of the UAW is one of the major sources of hope. Dictatorial power can always implement changes faster, but one problem in introducing changes, particularly work force management changes, is moving too fast; it's important that actions be thought out very carefully. To the extent to which a union can participate and help guide changes, management has an easier task. We know from past experience that things done rapidly by fiat are often ill-conceived.

Without trying to be oversolicitous of the UAW, its presence (depending of course on the local situation) is in general a definite plus factor. In my opinion the new auto contracts are very forward looking. We can contrast this situation with that in England, where the British have been unable to solve the class problems dividing management and the work force. We don't have those substantial barriers in the United States and should be able to solve our problems through management and labor working together to move forward. I'm bullish on the idea that a constructive relationship can be established between the work force's choice of bargaining unit and the auto industry. In spite of the fact that I teach at a business school, I believe that one of the greatest problems in this economy is the general decline of labor union membership since the 1950s.

SECREST: For myself, and I think I speak for many on the management side of this issue, the concept of more effective participation by workers in taking responsibility for quality and other factors offers considerable hope for the industry. This may be especially true if there is an effective sharing of leadership with the work force to stimulate the less active or less outgoing members. When we're all in the lifeboats together, the availability of a strong, democratic, concerned local union leadership can be a great help. This is not necessarily true in every instance, of course, any more than local management will always be enlightened enough to recognize what needs to be done.

MICHIGAN PAPERS IN JAPANESE STUDIES

Printed and bound by CPI Group (UK) Ltd, Croydon, CR0 4YY

14/04/2025

14656912-0001